C. B. Griesbach

HISTORIC ORNAMENT
A Pictorial Archive

900 FINE EXAMPLES FROM ANCIENT EGYPT TO 1800
SUITABLE FOR REPRODUCTION

DOVER PUBLICATIONS, INC.
New York

Published in Canada by General Publishing Company, Ltd., 30 Lesmill Road, Don Mills, Toronto,
Ontario.
Published in the United Kingdom by Constable
and Company, Ltd., 10 Orange Street, London WC 2.

Historic Ornament: A Pictorial Archive, first published by Dover Publications, Inc., in 1975, contains
280 plates from the portfolio *Muster-Ornamente
aus allen Stilen in historischer Anordnung*, originally
published by C. B. Griesbach in Gera, Germany,
n.d. [late nineteenth century]. The captions have
been translated into English specially for the present
edition.

DOVER *Pictorial Archive* SERIES

International Standard Book Number: 0-486-23215-8
Library of Congress Catalog Card Number: 75-12174

Manufactured in the United States of America
Dover Publications, Inc.
180 Varick Street
New York, N.Y. 10014

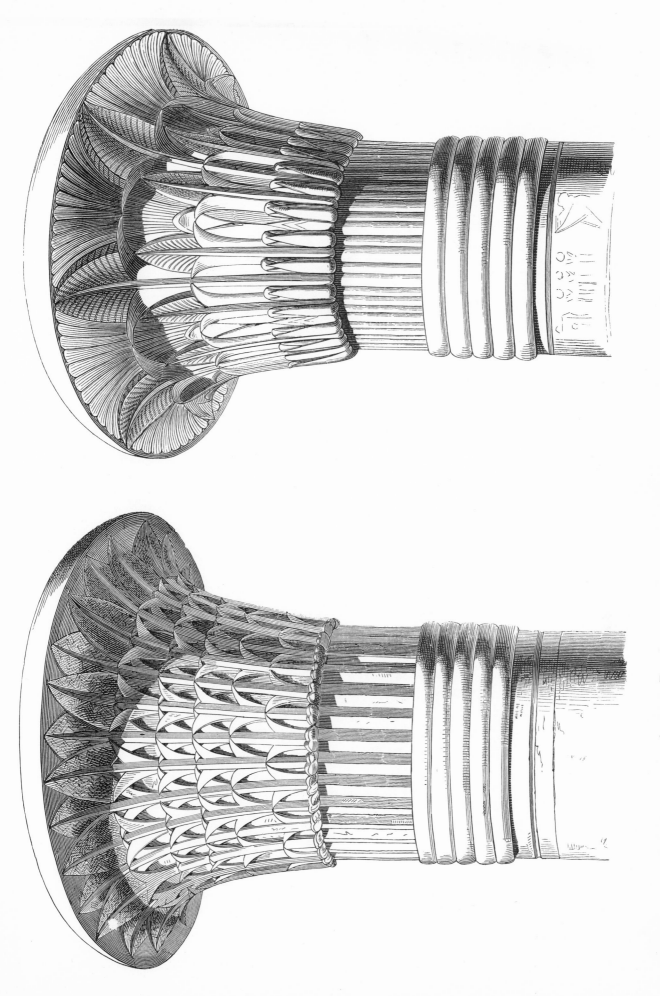

1 LEFT: Egyptian capital from the temple at Philae. RIGHT: Egyptian capital from the temple at Isna.

2   From Greek painted vases.

3 From Greek painted vases.

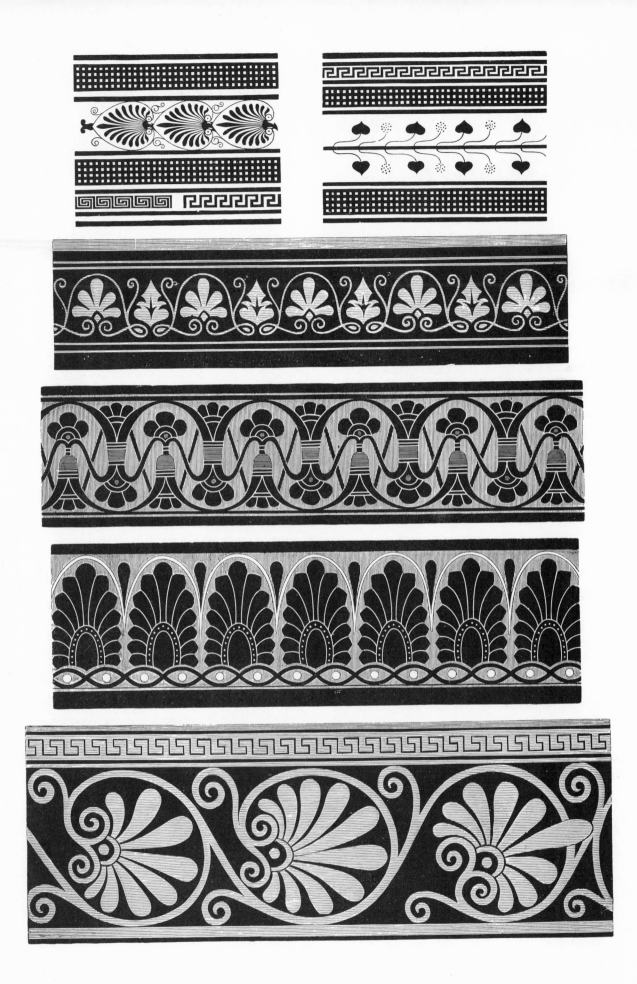

4 From Greek painted vases.

5   From Greek painted vases.

6 From Greek painted vases.

7 From Greek painted vases.

8 From Greek painted vases.

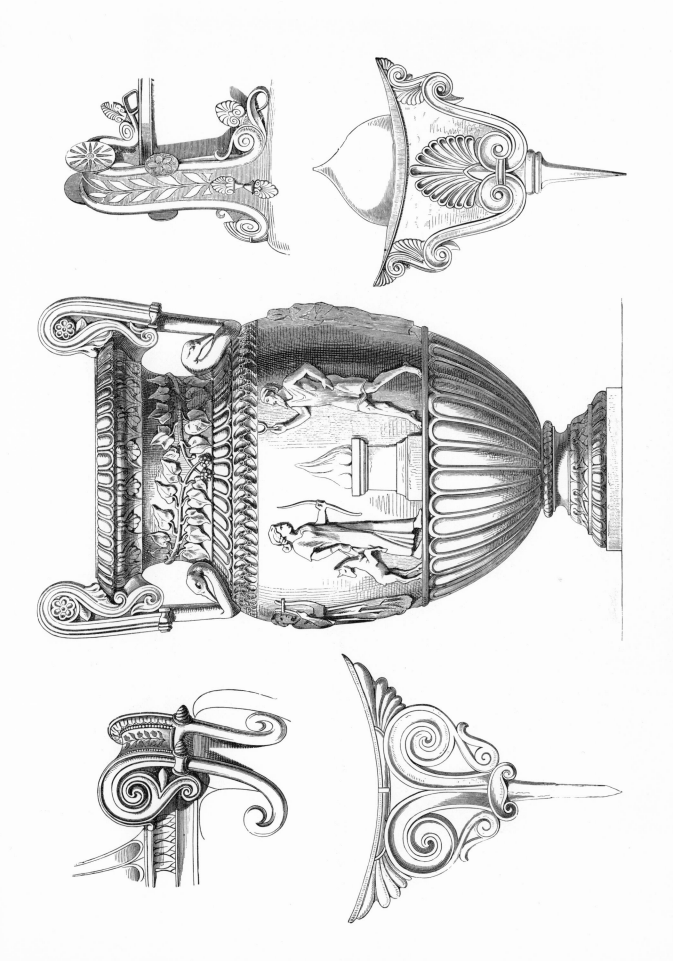

9 CENTER: Ancient Athenian vase by Sosibios in the Louvre, Paris. CORNERS: Motifs from ancient vessels and utensils.

10 ABOVE: Greek acroteria (roof finials). BELOW: Greek frieze of palmettes.

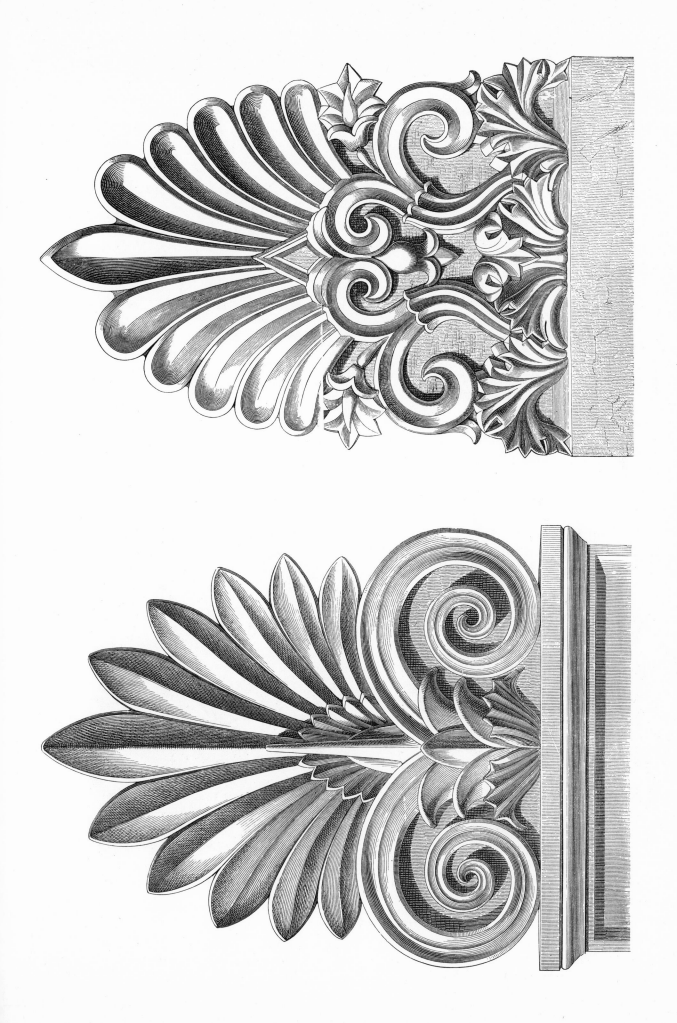

11 LEFT: Finial of a Greek stele. RIGHT: Antefix (upright eaves tile) from the Propylaea in Athens.

12 ABOVE LEFT: Antefix from the Propylaea in Athens. ABOVE RIGHT: Antefix from the Parthenon in Athens. BELOW LEFT: Finial of a Greek stele. BELOW RIGHT: Greco-Roman terra-cotta antefix.

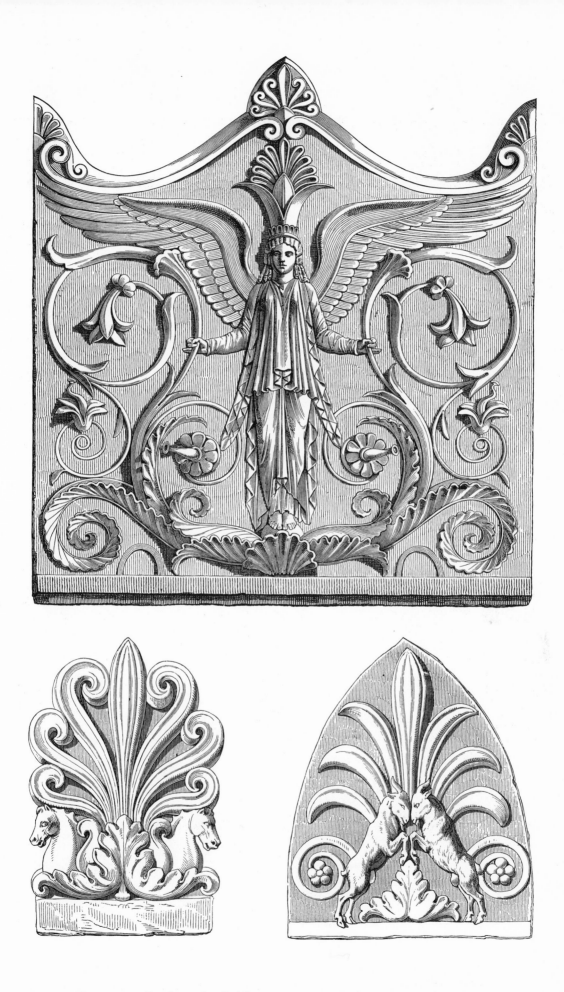

13　ABOVE: Greek cornice finial. BELOW: Greco-Roman terra-cotta antefixes.

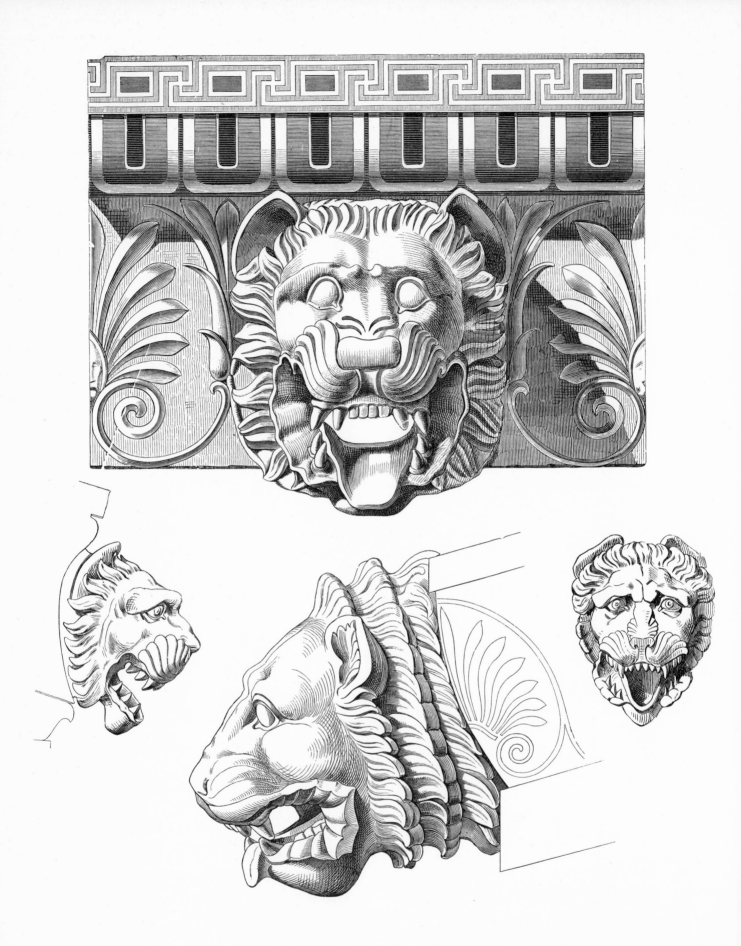

14 ABOVE: Painted terra-cotta sima (roof gutter molding) from a Doric temple in Metapontum. BELOW, CENTER: Lion's head from the Parthenon in Athens. BELOW, SIDES: Side and front views of a lion's head from Selinus, Sicily.

15   Greco-Roman terra-cotta sima (ABOVE) and frieze (BELOW).

16   ABOVE: Finial of the choragic monument of Lysicrates in Athens. BELOW: Greek
ornament from the Erechtheion in Athens. SIDES: Front and side views of a lintel
console from the Erechtheion.

17 ABOVE: Greek capital from an engaged column inside the temple of Apollo Didymaeus near Miletus. BELOW: Greek acanthus leaf from the capital of the Tower of the Winds in Athens.

18 Front view, ground plan and cross section of an Etruscan terra-cotta antefix in the Perugia museum.

19 Two views of a Roman marble vase.

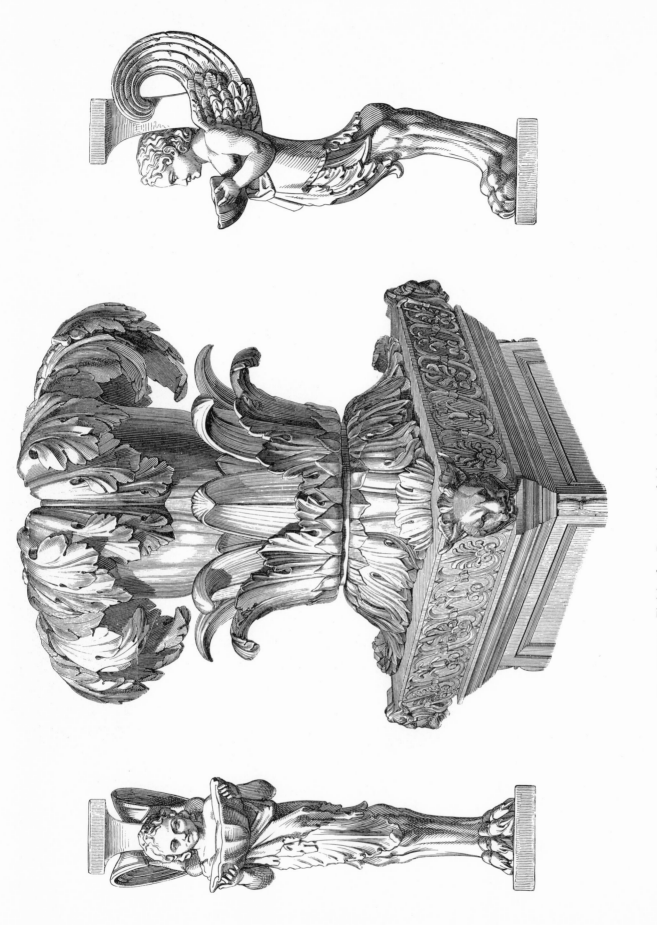

20 CENTER: Finial of a Roman candelabrum in the Vatican Museum, Rome. SIDES: Front and side views of a marble table-leg from Pompeii.

21 Roman carved astragals and rosette from the temple of Jupiter Tonans in Rome.

22   ABOVE: Roman capital in the Louvre, Paris. BELOW: Roman Ionic capital.

23   ABOVE: Rosette from the Forum of Nerva in Rome. BELOW: Fragment of a keystone from the Forum of Trajan in Rome.

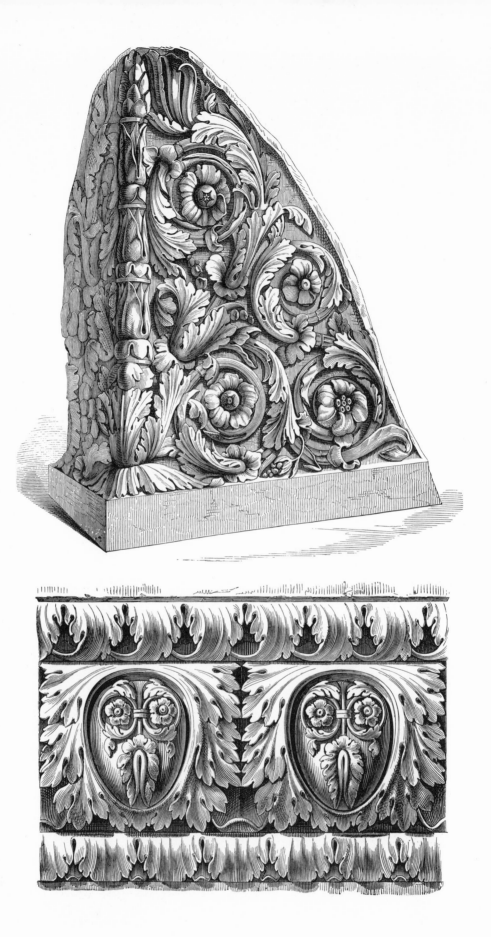

24 ABOVE: Roman marble corner acroterion in the Villa Pamfili, Rome. BELOW: Roman decorative egg-and-tongue molding.

25   Front and side views of a Roman Ionic capital.

26 TOP AND CENTER: Frieze from the temple of Antoninus and Faustina in the Forum Romanum. BOTTOM: Roman marble panel.

27　ABOVE: Architrave ornament from the temple of Jupiter Stator in Rome. BELOW: Roman molding with bead-and-reel motif.

28 ABOVE: Roman antefix. BELOW: Roman frieze.

29 TOP: Sima from the temple of Jupiter Tonans in Rome. CENTER: Corner of a Roman frieze. BOTTOM: Roman molding with egg-and-dart and bead-and-reel elements.

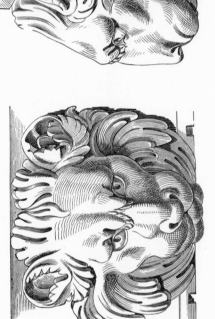

30 ABOVE CENTER: Corinthian capital from the House of the Labyrinth in Pompeii. ABOVE LEFT: Two views of a console in the Vatican Museum. ABOVE RIGHT: Two views of a Roman Corinthian cornice console. BELOW: Front and side views of a lion's head from the temple of Antoninus and Faustina in Rome.

31 Vessels from the Hildesheim hoard of silver (Roman).

32 Details of vessels from the Hildesheim hoard.

33 Objects from the Hildesheim hoard.

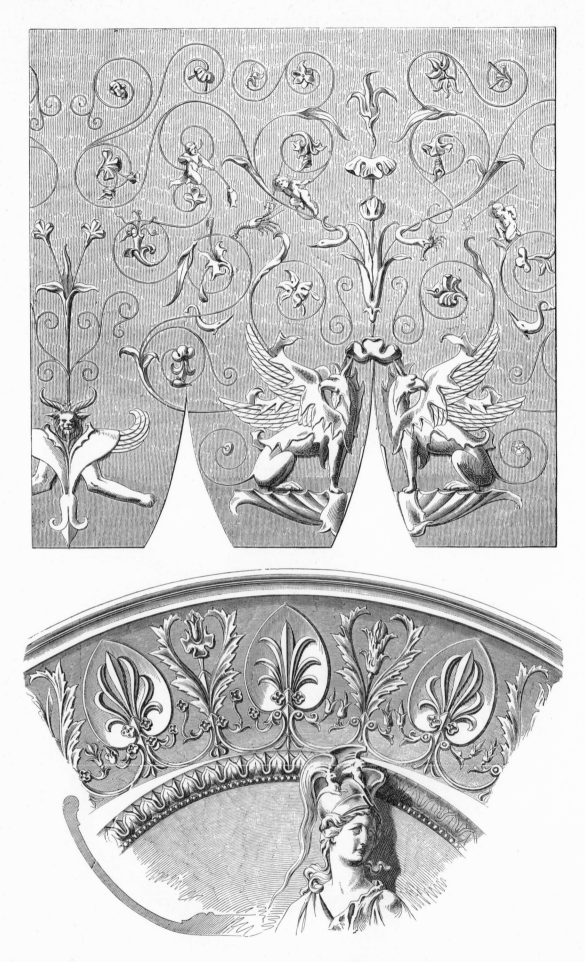

34 Objects from the Hildesheim hoard.

35 Vessels from the Hildesheim hoard.

36 FROM TOP TO BOTTOM: Byzantine ornamentation on tie beams of St. Sophia in
Istanbul; Byzantine ornament from St. Mark's in Venice; Byzantine ornament from
the church of the Hormisdas monastery, Agios Sergios, Istanbul; ornament from
an early Christian sarcophagus in the basilica of S. Apollinare in Classe near
Ravenna.

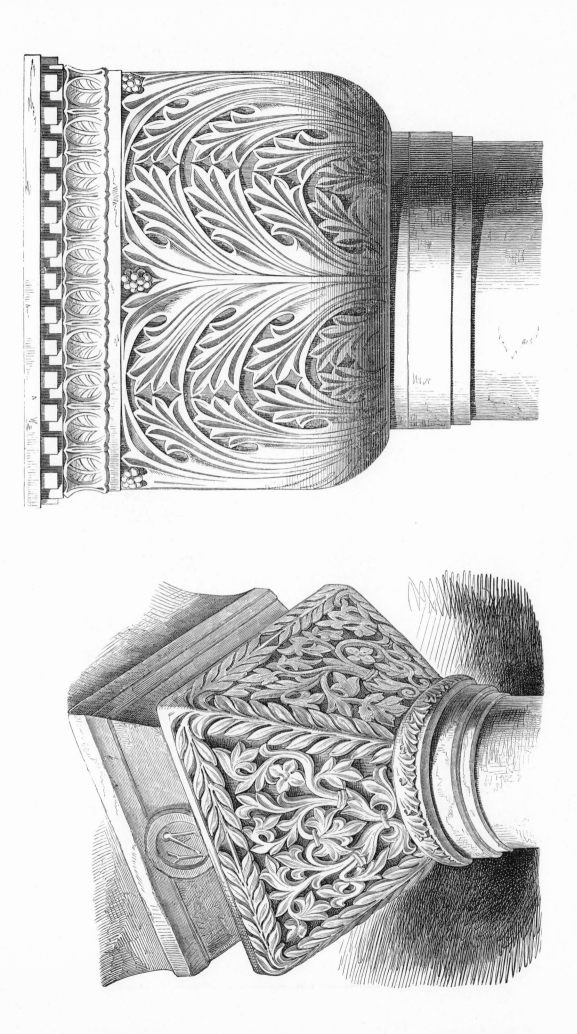

37 LEFT: Byzantine capital in the choir of S. Vitale in Ravenna. RIGHT: Byzantine capital from the church of S. Sofia in Padua.

38 Byzantine mosaic ornaments from St. Sophia in Istanbul.

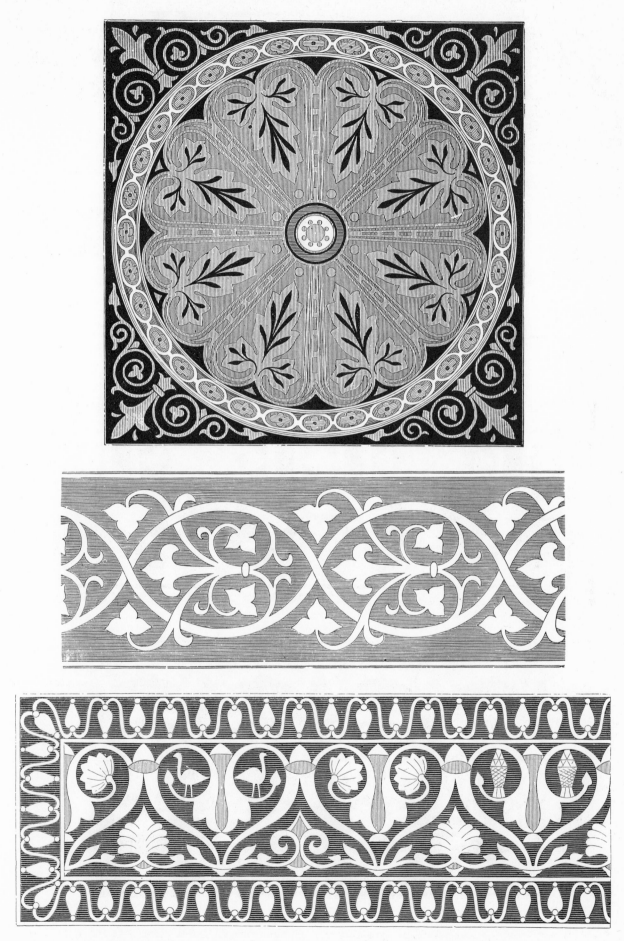

39 Byzantine glass-mosaic ornaments from St. Mark's in Venice (TOP AND CENTER) and St. Sophia in Istanbul (BOTTOM).

40   TOP: Two early Christian mosaics from S. Giovanni a Porta Latina, Rome. CENTER AND BOTTOM: Mosaic decorations from the Monreale cathedral near Palermo (1174–1186).

41 FROM TOP TO BOTTOM: Persian ornaments in the British Museum, London (the two right-angled items and the three items they enclose); gold ornament on an Oriental weapon in a Vienna museum; carved wooden bar from the door of an old palace in Ceylon, now in the Victoria and Albert Museum, London.

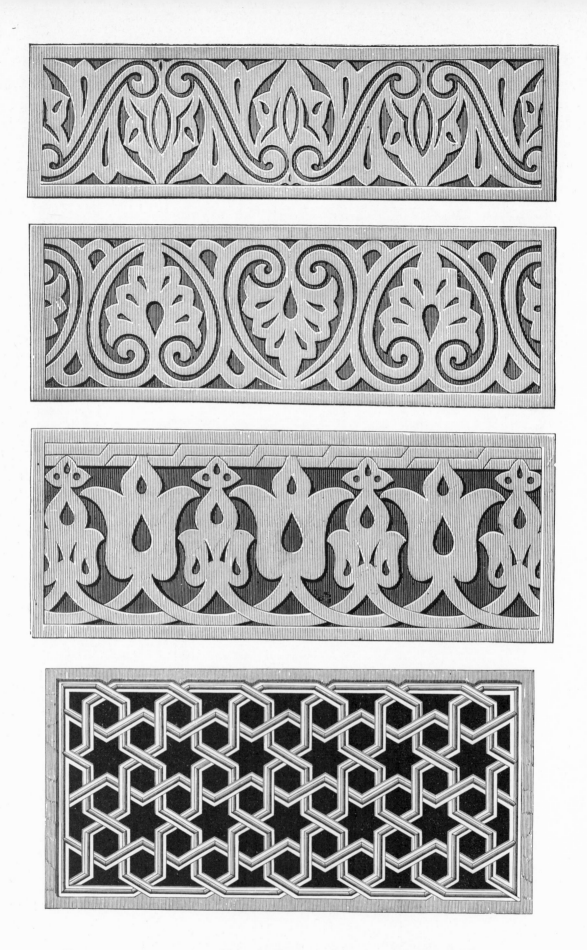

42 FROM TOP TO BOTTOM: Three Arabic stucco decorations from the El Mas mosque
in Cairo (11th century); Arabic window grille in the mosque of Hakim in Cairo
(11th century).

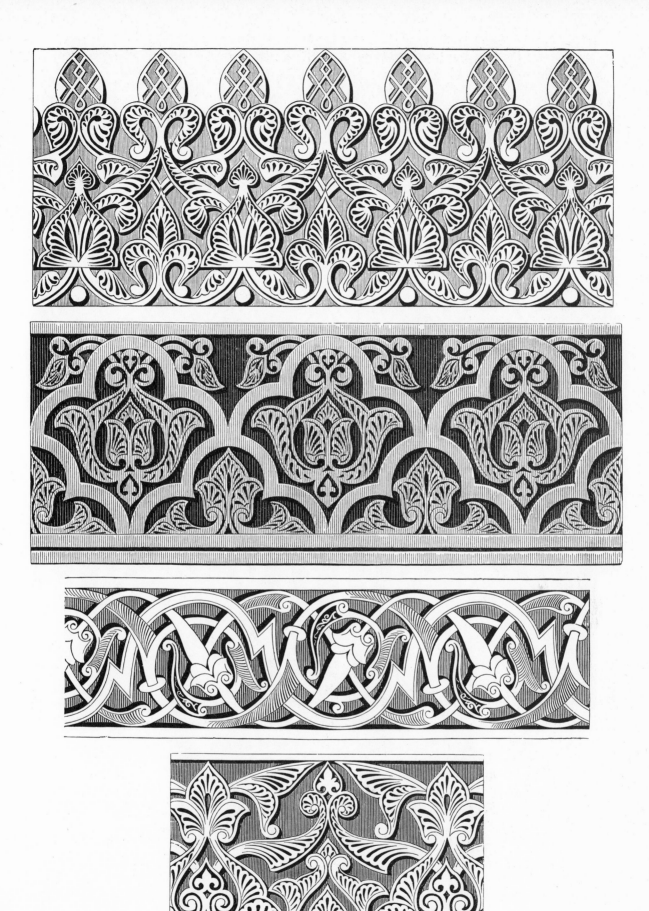

43   Arabic ornaments from 13th-century mosques in Cairo.

44   ABOVE: Two Arabic ornaments from the mosque of Kaloon in Cairo (13th century). BELOW: Painted panels from the exposed rafters of the cathedral of Messina (1130).

45　Arabic ornaments of the 13th century.

46 Arabic ornaments from Cairo (13th century).

47 ABOVE: Arabic ornament from the Great Mosque in Damascus (14th century).
BELOW: Arabic frieze from the Omu mosque in Cairo (14th century).

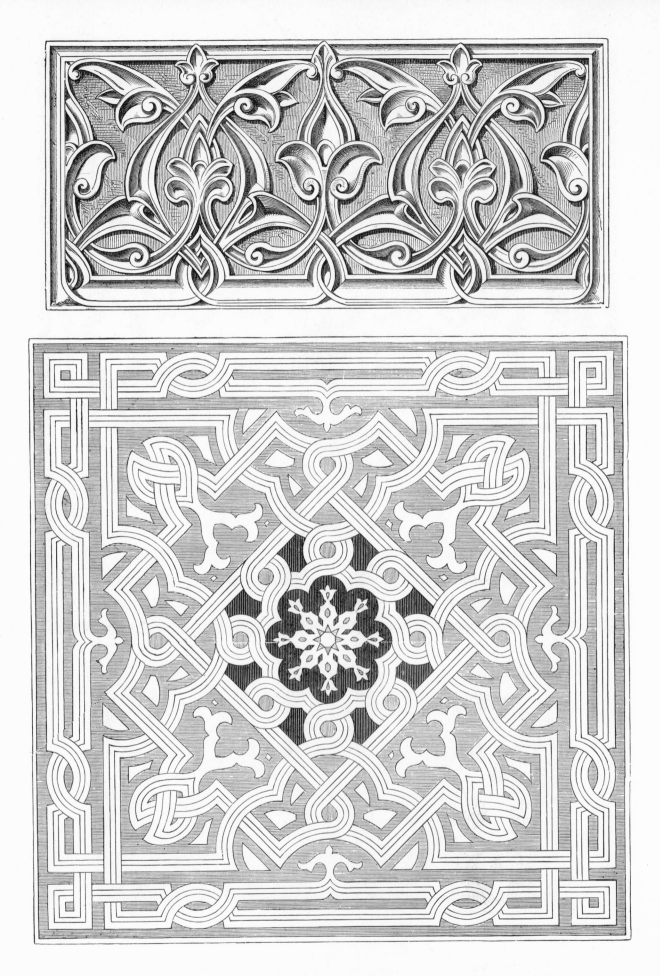

48 Arabic ornaments from the mosque of Sultan Hassan in Cairo (14th century).

49 ABOVE: Arabic ornament from the mosque of Sultan Hassan in Cairo (14th century). BELOW LEFT: Moorish panel from the Sala del Barca in the Alhambra (14th century). BELOW RIGHT: Ornament from the inner face of an arch in the Hall of the Abencerages in the Alhambra (14th century).

50   Moorish ornaments from the Alhambra (14th century).

51 ABOVE, AND BELOW LEFT: Moorish ornaments from the Alhambra (14th century).
BELOW RIGHT: Moorish battle-axe from the Alhambra.

52   Moorish ornaments from the Alhambra (14th century).

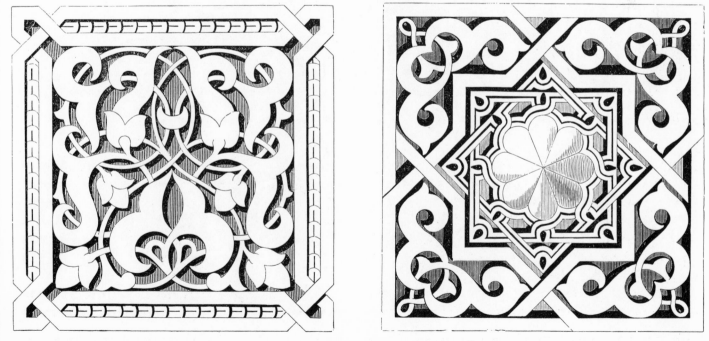

53 Moorish ornaments from the Alhambra (14th century).

54   Moorish ornaments from the Alhambra (14th century).

55 TOP: Mosaic from Cairo, in black and white marble with red bricks. CENTER AND
BOTTOM: Arabic ornaments from the mausoleum of Sultan Chairbek in Cairo (early
16th century).

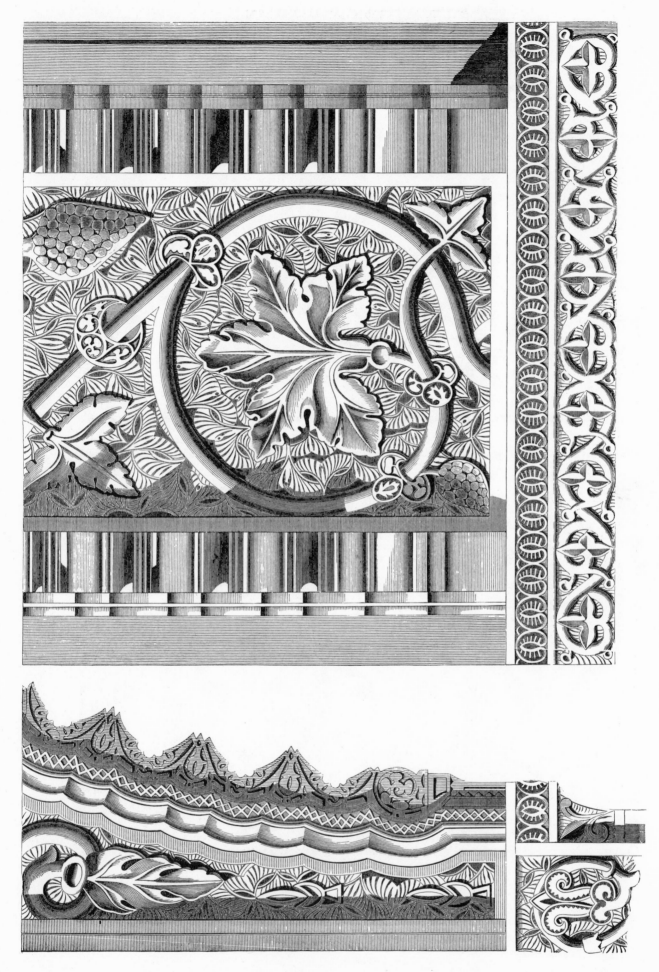

56 Front and side views of the abutment and arch in the hall of the Mesa house in Toledo, in the *mudéjar* (Moorish-Christian) style (14th century).

57 Ceiling painting in the Palatine Chapel in Palermo.

58 Mosaic border from the central apse of St. Mark's in Venice.

57 Ceiling painting in the Palatine Chapel in Palermo.

58 Mosaic border from the central apse of St. Mark's in Venice.

59 Mosaic bands from St. Mark's in Venice.

60   Romanesque capital and frieze from the Prefecture in Angers (11th century).

61   ABOVE: Two Romanesque panels from the cloister of the Prefecture in Angers (11th
century). BELOW: Romanesque arched frame of the rose window of the transept of
Notre-Dame in Châlons-sur-Marne.

62 CENTER: Romanesque altar candlestick of gilt bronze in the church at Comburg, Württemberg (12th century). SIDES: Romanesque knockers.

63 TOP: Tympanum of the Naumburg cathedral (12th century). CENTRAL ROW,
EXTREME LEFT AND RIGHT: Bosses from the chapter house of the Heiligenkreuz
monastery near Vienna (13th century). CENTRAL ROW, CENTER: Rosette from the
portal of the north transept of the Amiens cathedral (13th century). BOTTOM: Tympanum of St. Michael's in Schwäbisch Hall (12th century).

64 TOP: Romanesque portal ornament from the Bonn cathedral. CENTER LEFT: Romanesque capital in the Germanisches Museum in Nuremberg. CENTER RIGHT: Romanesque capital from the Schottenkirche (St. James') in Regensburg (12th century). BOTTOM: Romanesque abutment decoration in the Mainz cathedral.

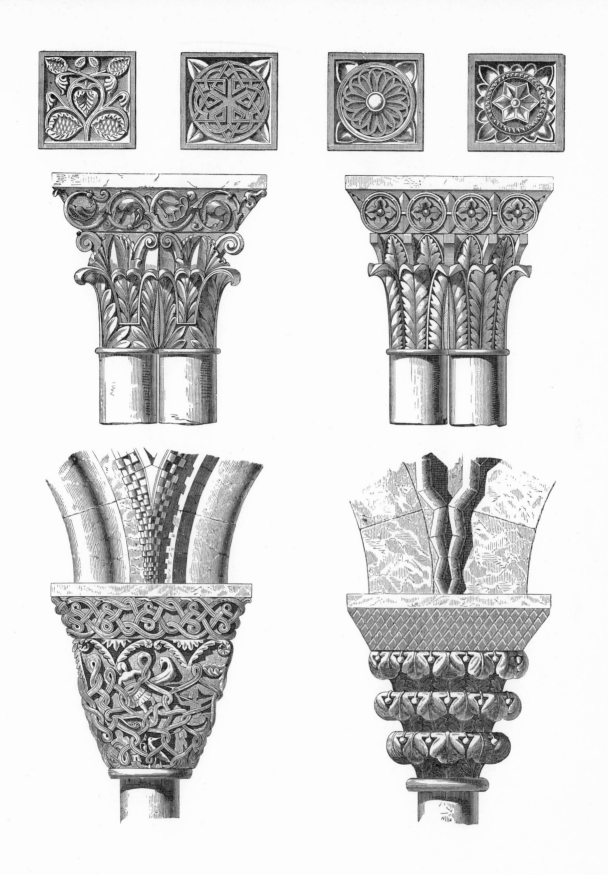

65 TOP: Four rosettes located between the consoles of the portal lintel of St Lawrence's
in Segovia (12th century). CENTER: Two capitals from St. Martin's in Segovia
(12th century). BOTTOM: Capitals and archivolts in the narthex (vestibule) of St.
Lawrence's in Segovia.

66 ABOVE: Tympanum of a portal (now walled up) in Worms (12th century).
BELOW: Tympanum of the south transept of St. Martin's in Worms (11th century).

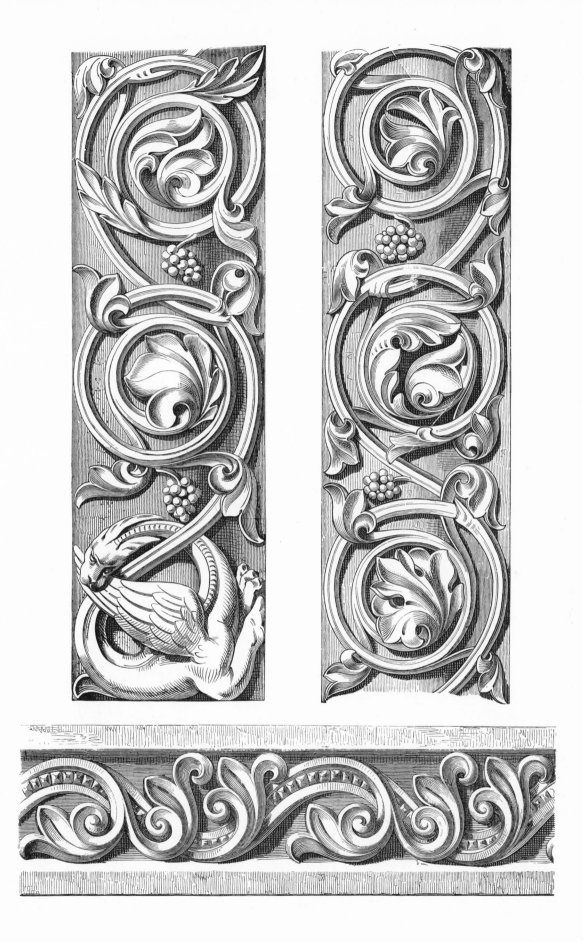

67 ABOVE: Two Romanesque ornaments from the portal of the collegiate church in Aschaffenburg (12th century). BELOW: Romanesque ornament of the 12th century.

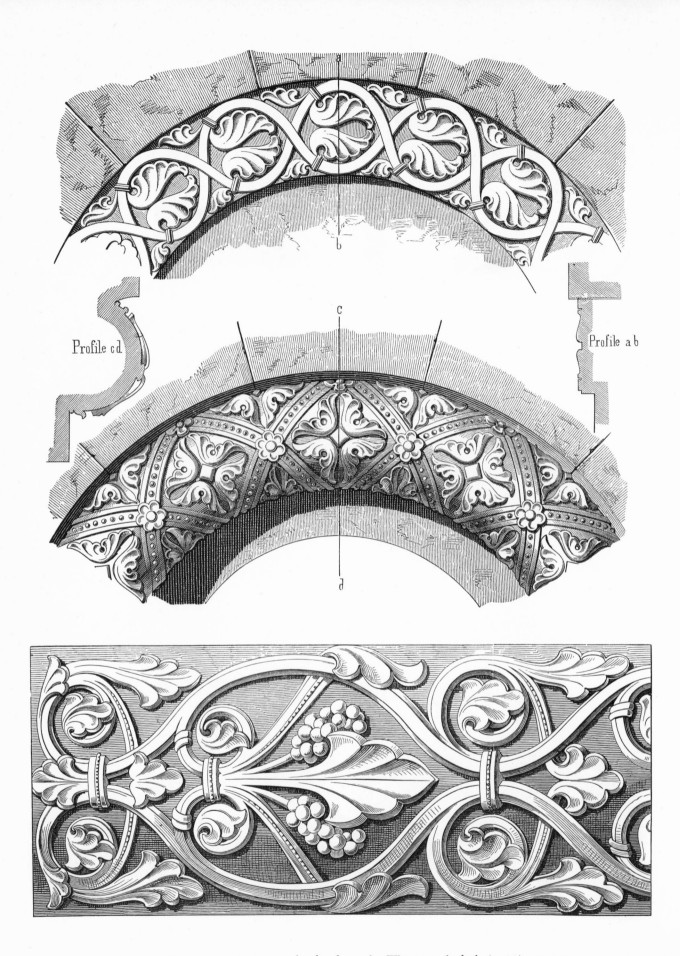

Profile c d

Profile a b

68 TOP: Romanesque tympanum border from the Worms cathedral (1110). CENTER
AND BOTTOM: Romanesque ornaments from the church at Gelnhausen (early 13th
century).

69   ABOVE: Romanesque capital from the collegiate church in Aschaffenburg. BELOW: Ornament on the arch of the west portal of the monastery church Marienberg near Helmstedt (12th century).

70   TOP: Romanesque plinth from the Bonn cathedral. CENTER: Border of a Romanesque gravestone in Sankt Maria auf dem Kapitol in Cologne. BOTTOM: Romanesque abutment cornice from Münzenberg, Hesse (12th century).

71 TOP: Romanesque ornament of the 12th century. CENTER: Romanesque column-
shaft ornament from Büchenberg near Goslar (12th century). BOTTOM: Romanesque frieze from the citadel in Münzenberg.

72 ABOVE: Two Romanesque capitals from the collegiate church and the cloister in Aschaffenburg. BELOW: Two Romanesque capitals from the tower hall of St. George's in Dinkelsbühl (12th century).

73 ABOVE, AND BELOW CENTER: Romanesque frieze and capital, based on partially
destroyed originals found in Würzburg (12th century). BELOW, SIDES: Two bosses
from the cloister of St. Emmeram's in Regensburg (end of the 13th century).

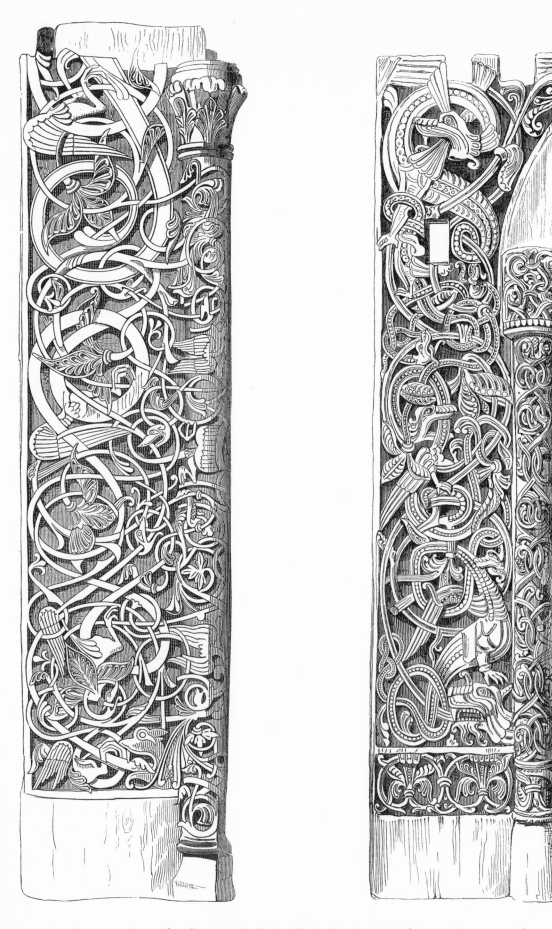

74 LEFT: One side of a portal of the Ulwig church at Hardanger, Norway (13th century). RIGHT: One side of a portal of the Stedye church in the Songdal monastery at Bergen, Norway.

75 Romanesque portal frame from the Lucca cathedral.

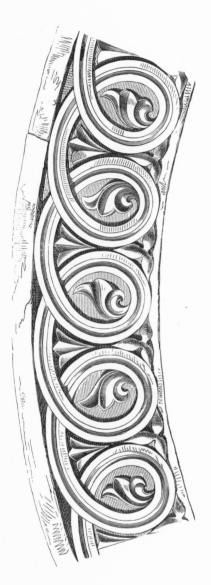

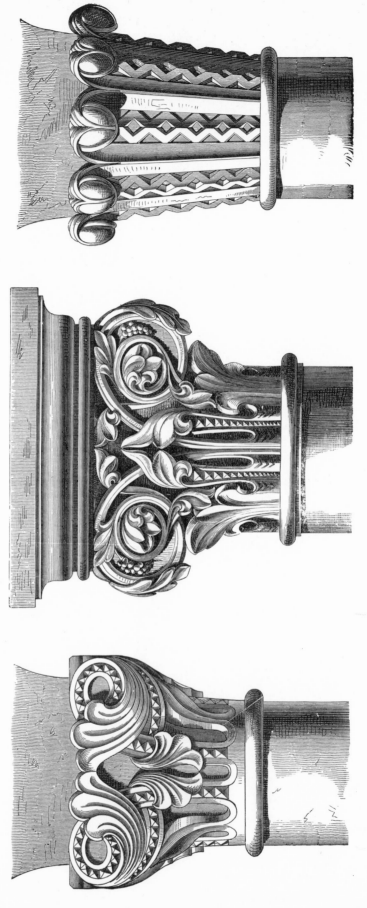

76 ABOVE: Arch ornament on the gate of a Romanesque house in Regensburg. BELOW, LEFT TO RIGHT: Romanesque capital from the narthex of the collegiate church in Aschaffenburg (12th century); two Romanesque capitals from the church at Seegringen, Bavaria (12th century).

77 Capitals and keystones from the monastery church in Drübeck near Wernigerode
(12th century).

78 TOP LEFT: Capital of an engaged column in the narthex of the collegiate church in Ellwangen, Württemberg (13th century). TOP RIGHT: Capital of a free-standing pillar in the church at Brenz, Württemberg (12th century). CENTER: Romanesque coupled capitals in the cathedral of St. George in Limburg an der Lahn (13th century). BOTTOM: Capitals in Romanesque style from the church at Schwarzrheindorf near Bonn (12th century).

79   ABOVE: Romanesque panel in the church at Schwarzrheindorf (mid-12th century).
BELOW: Two capitals from partially engaged columns on the north portals of the
Bamberg cathedral (13th century).

80 Romanesque ceiling paintings in St. Michael's, Hildesheim (early 13th century).

81   Paintings on pedestals in the upper church at Assisi (13th century).

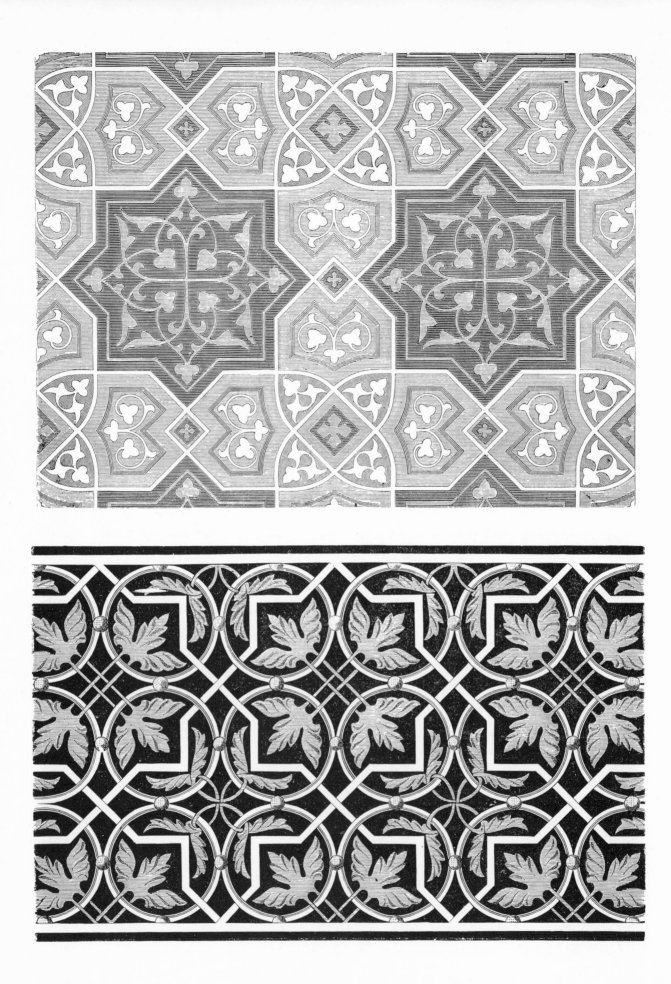

82   Wall paintings from S. Francesco in Assisi (13th century).

83 ABOVE: Terra-cotta tile from the church at Bloxham, England (15th century).
BELOW: Tiles from the Cistercian monastery, Bebenhausen, Württemberg.

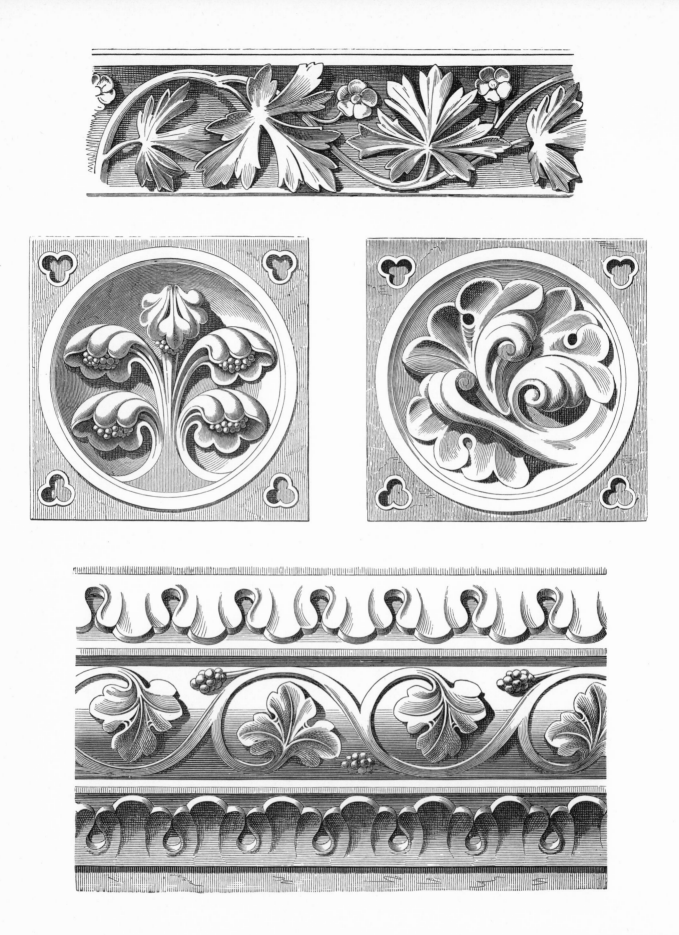

84 TOP: Early Gothic frieze from Chartres (13th century). CENTER: Two early Gothic rosettes from the entrance to the Séez (Orne) cathedral (13th century). BOTTOM: Early Gothic ornamental element of the column bases of the narthex of the Sens cathedral.

85 Ornaments from Notre-Dame, Paris (13th century).

86 ABOVE: Chief cornice of the aisle in the Laon cathedral (13th century). BELOW:
Panel on the pedestal of a pillar of the Porte Rouge, Notre-Dame, Paris.

87　ABOVE: Early Gothic ornament from the west portal of Notre-Dame, Paris (early 13th century). BELOW: Early Gothic pillar capital of the 13th century.

88   Cornice and capital from Notre-Dame, Paris (13th century).

89 ABOVE: Two bosses from the Sainte-Chapelle, Paris (13th century). BELOW: Early Gothic frieze from Notre-Dame, Paris.

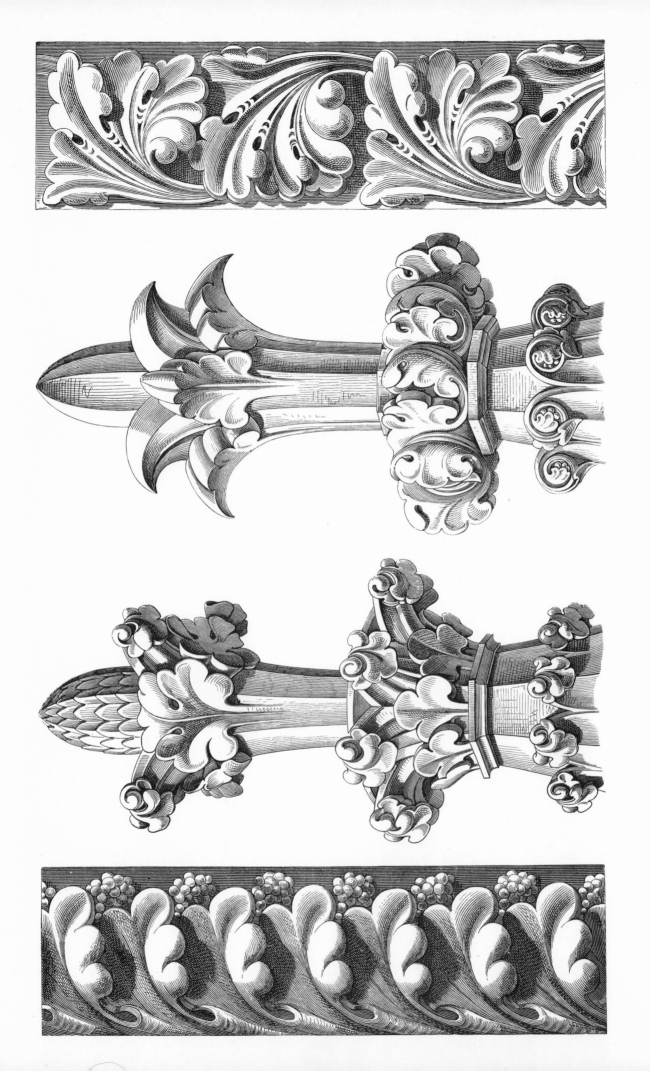

90 LEFT AND RIGHT: Ornaments in grooves between the narthex columns in the abbey of Larchand (13th century). CENTER: Two finials from the south tower of the Chartres cathedral (13th century).

91 ABOVE: Early Gothic lintel ornament from the north narthex of the Chartres
cathedral (13th century). BELOW: Early Gothic overdoor from the lower church
of the Sainte-Chapelle, Paris.

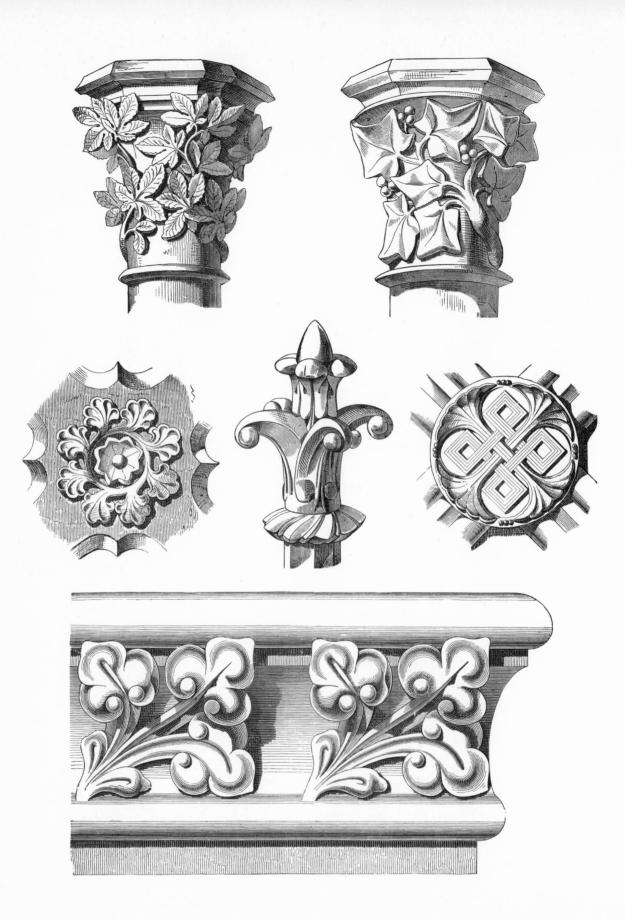

92 TOP: Two capitals from the church of Sts. Peter and Paul at Wimpfen im Thale (13th century). CENTRAL ROW, EXTREME LEFT AND RIGHT: Bosses from the Regensburg and Basel cathedrals. CENTRAL ROW, CENTER: Finial on the highest divisions of the doors of Notre-Dame, Paris (13th century). BOTTOM: Cornice of the choir enclosure of Notre-Dame, Paris (13th century).

93 ABOVE: Gothic ornament in a groove of the south door of the church at Friedberg, Hesse (14th century). BELOW: Gothic groove ornament from Notre-Dame, Paris (early 14th century).

94 LEFT: Capital from the Naumburg cathedral (13th century). RIGHT: Capital from the Aschaffenburg cloister (13th century).

95 ABOVE: Frieze from St. Peter's in Lisieux. BELOW: Gothic cornice from the chapel of Louis IX in the Sainte-Chapelle, Paris.

96 TOP: Gothic ornament from the font of St. Mary's in Reutlingen (15th century). CENTER: Two Gothic capitals from partially engaged columns in the belfry of the Frauenkirche at Esslingen (15th century). BOTTOM: Gothic openwork frieze in St. Mary's, Lübeck (15th century).

97   TOP: Two Gothic finials from the choir of the Chartres cathedral. CENTER: Gothic door frame from the church of San Juan de los Reyes, Toledo (15th century). BOTTOM: Gothic ornament from the church at Batalha, Portugal.

98 CENTER: Panel from the Gothic choir stalls in the cathedral of Tarnow, Galicia
(15th century). LEFT AND RIGHT: Frieze ornaments from a wardrobe in the church
at Nördlingen (late 16th century).

99   LEFT AND RIGHT: Gothic carvings on the rafters of the main room of the Über-
lingen town hall (15th century). CENTER: Late Gothic ornament on an altar coffer
in the parish church at Weissenburg am Sand.

100 TOP: Panel ornament from a Gothic altar in the church of St. Aegidius in Bartfeld, Hungary (1499). CENTER: Three Gothic rosettes from the choir stalls of the Ulm cathedral (15th century). BOTTOM: Wooden console from the high altar of St. Mary's, Krakow, carved by Veit Stoss (16th century).

101   FROM TOP TO BOTTOM: Hem of the robe of a wooden statue on the high altar of
St. Kilian's in Heilbronn (15th century); three Gothic ornaments carved in wood
by Master Cuonrat of Ravensburg in 1429.

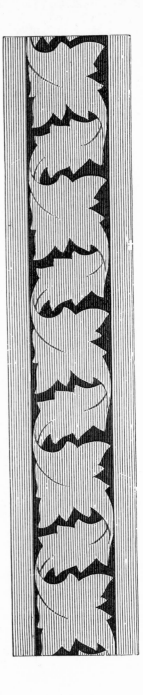

102   LEFT AND RIGHT: Low-relief wood carvings of the late 15th century. CENTER: Late Gothic low-relief wood carving from one side of the octagonal pulpit in the graveyard chapel at Wimpfen im Thale (16th century).

103 ABOVE: Low-relief wood carving of the late 15th century. BELOW: Three late
Gothic wood carvings in the monastery church at Hirsau and the church at Alten-
burg near Calw, Württemberg (15th century).

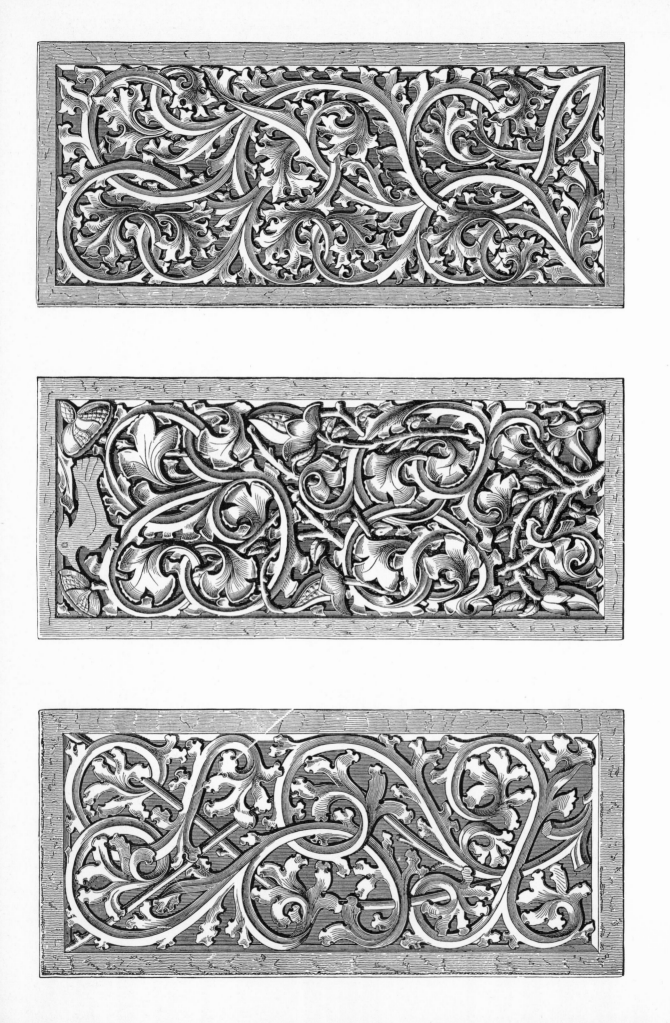

104 Panels from the Gothic choir stalls in the cathedral of Tarnow, Galicia (15th century).

105 Pattern on the robe of a statue on a bishop's monument in the Freising cathedral (13th century).

106   Gothic textile patterns (14th century).

107   Vestment pattern of the 14th century. From a collection of vestments of the former Kalander brotherhood at Stralsund, in the Stralsund provincial museum.

108 Vestment pattern of the 14th century. From the Stralsund collection.

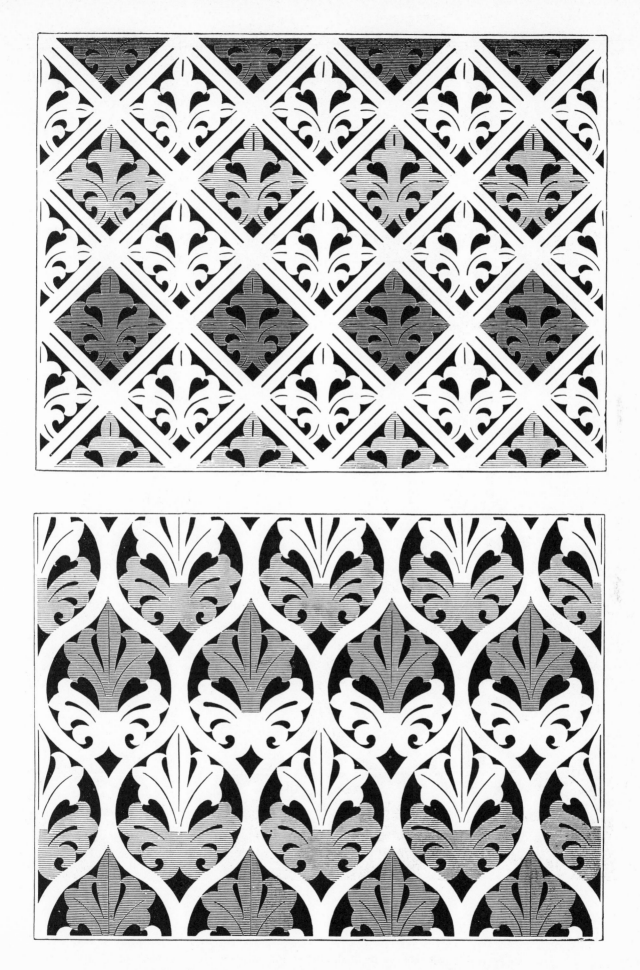

109   Stencil painting on a Brandenburg wardrobe (early 15th century).

110   Gothic textile pattern from the high altar of the main church in Rothenburg (15th century).

111 Patterns from the backgrounds of paintings and from altar coffers of the 15th century.

112 Textile patterns of the 15th century.

113 TOP: Border of a book cover, stamped on parchment (1543). CENTER: Textile
pattern from the Halberstadt cathedral. BOTTOM: Mosaic from St. Mark's in Venice.

114 ABOVE LEFT: Gothic chalice in the treasury of the Krakow cathedral. ABOVE RIGHT: Gothic chalice in St. Mary's, Krakow. BELOW: Ornament from a Gothic Communion cup in the treasury of the Tarnow cathedral, Galicia.

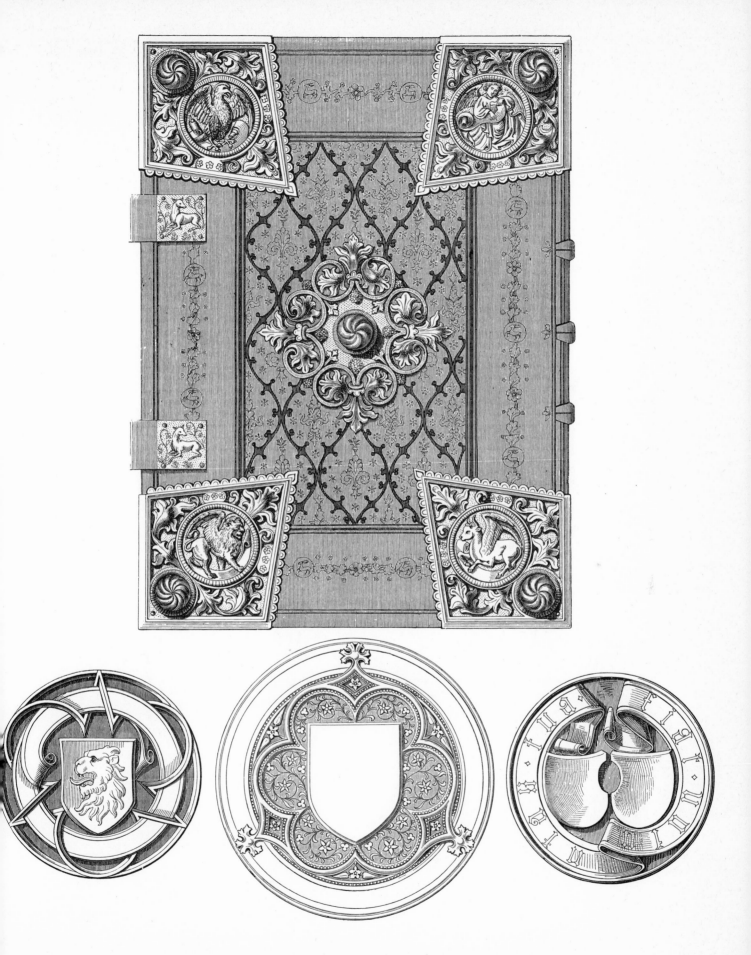

115 ABOVE: Late Gothic binding of a German Bible printed in 1472. BELOW: Coat-of-arms of the 15th century.

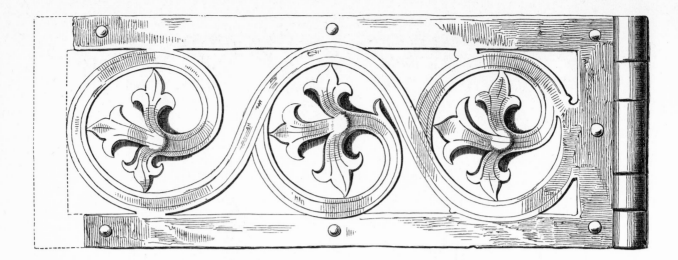

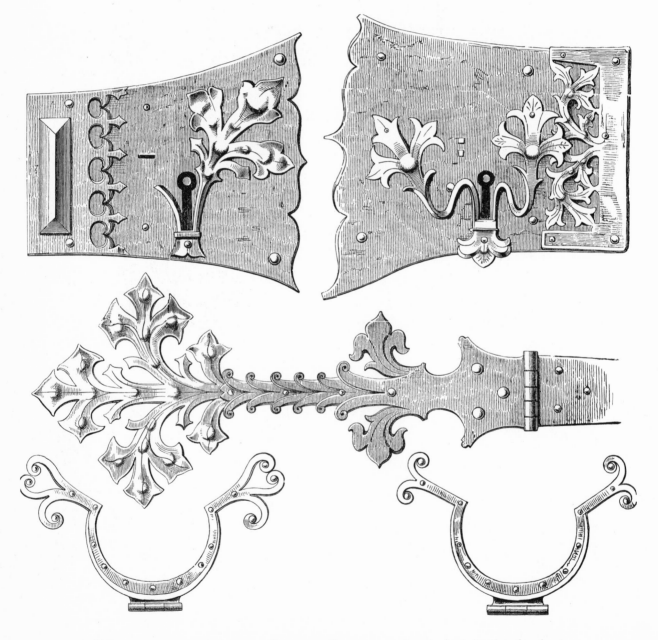

116   TOP AND CENTER RIGHT: Iron mounting on a vestment chest in the church at Kiedrich (15th century). CENTER LEFT AND JUST BELOW: Bronze mounting on a prayer desk in Gelnhausen (15th century). BOTTOM: Door fittings from the church at Dietkirchen, Nassau.

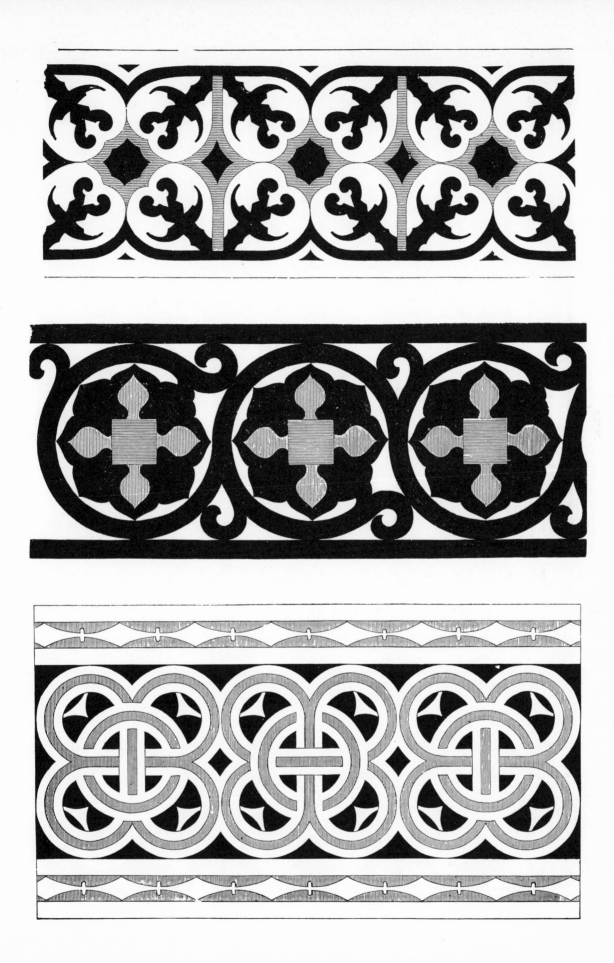

117 Italian Gothic mosaic ornaments from the cathedral, S. Croce and the Baptistery in Florence.

118   Italian Gothic. ABOVE: Marble floor in the Milan cathedral. BELOW: Mosaic from
S. Croce in Florence.

119   ABOVE: Marble mosaic floor in the tabernacle of the church of Orsanmichele in Florence (1348). BELOW: Sections of the Italian Gothic marble mosaic floor in the Lucca cathedral (1204).

120   Italian Gothic. ABOVE: Wall decoration in the Palazzo del Podestà, Florence (14th century). BELOW: Hem of a robe in S. Croce, Florence (14th century).

121   ABOVE: Sections of the wrought-iron grille of the funerary monument of the
della Scala family in Verona (14th century). BELOW: Italian Gothic wrought-iron
chapel grille in the Prato cathedral (15th century).

122   ABOVE: Capital from the lower row of columns in the Doge's Palace, Venice (15th century). BELOW: Italian Gothic coping of the choir wall behind the high altar of S. Maria della Catena, Palermo.

123   TOP LEFT AND RIGHT, AND BOTTOM LEFT: Marble vault consoles from the Ducal Palace, Urbino (15th century). CENTER AND BOTTOM RIGHT: Marble capitals from the charterhouse near Florence (15th century).

124 Ornaments from architecture by Filippo Brunelleschi (15th century).

125 Details from Benedetto da Maiano's pulpit in S. Croce, Florence (15th century).

126 ABOVE: Marble stoup in the Orvieto cathedral (15th century). BELOW: Frieze over the portal of S. Michele in Bosco, Bologna, by Peruzzi (early 16th century).

127 ABOVE: Marble panels from the Verona town hall (16th century). BELOW: Frieze
from the choir railing in S. Maria dei Miracoli, Venice (15th century).

128 ABOVE: Frieze with medallions in S. Maria della Pace, Rome, by Bramante of Urbino (1504). BELOW: Two Renaissance pilaster capitals in S. Maddalena de' Pazzi, Florence (late 15th century).

129   ABOVE: Frieze with medallions in S. Maria della Pace, Rome. BELOW LEFT: Marble pilaster capital in the sacristy of S. Spirito, Florence, by Filippo Brunelleschi (1385–1444). BELOW RIGHT: Pilaster capital in S. Maddalena de' Pazzi, Florence.

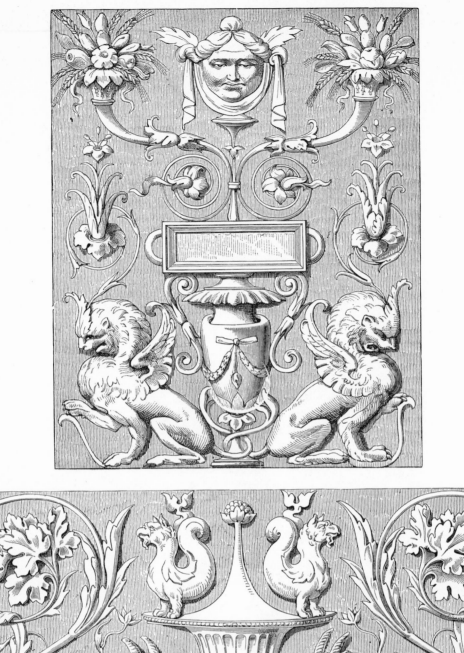

130 Panels from S. Maria dei Miracoli, Venice (15th century).

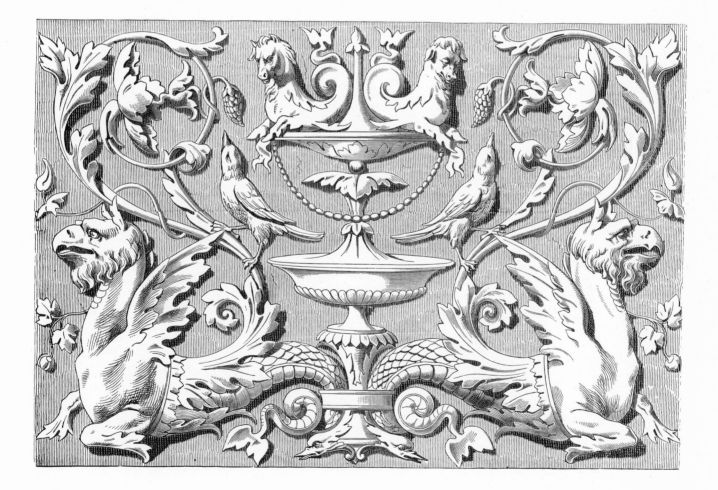

131   ABOVE: Italian Renaissance panel. BELOW: Marble panel from S. Maria dei Miracoli,
      Venice (15th century).

132 Pilaster capital with additional top element, from the triumphal arch in the choir
of S. Maria dei Miracoli, Venice (15th century).

133   Detail of the arcades over the Giant Stairway in the courtyard of the Doge's Palace, Venice (early 16th century).

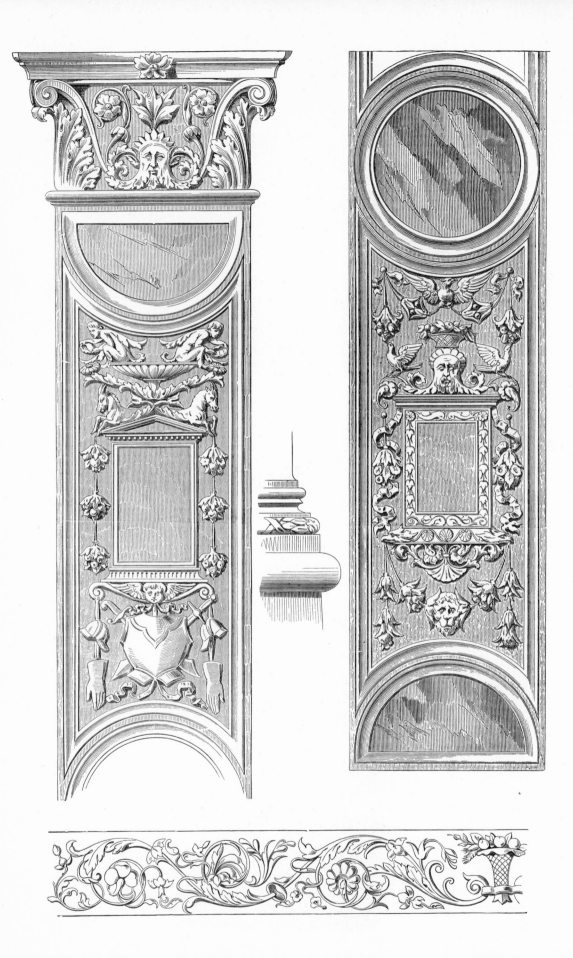

134 ABOVE: Italian Renaissance corner pilaster in the Palazzo de' Leoni, Ferrara. BELOW: Ornament by Andrea Sansovino (1460–1529).

135 CENTER: Italian Renaissance pilaster capital in the Casa Doria, Genoa. SIDES:
Pilaster panels by Baccio Pintelli in S. Agostino, Rome.

136 Capitals in the courtyard of the Scrofa palace, Ferrara (16th century).

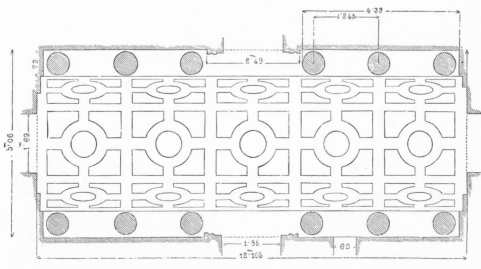

137 Coffer and plan of a barrel vault in the sacristy corridor of S. Spirito, Florence, by
Andrea Sansovino.

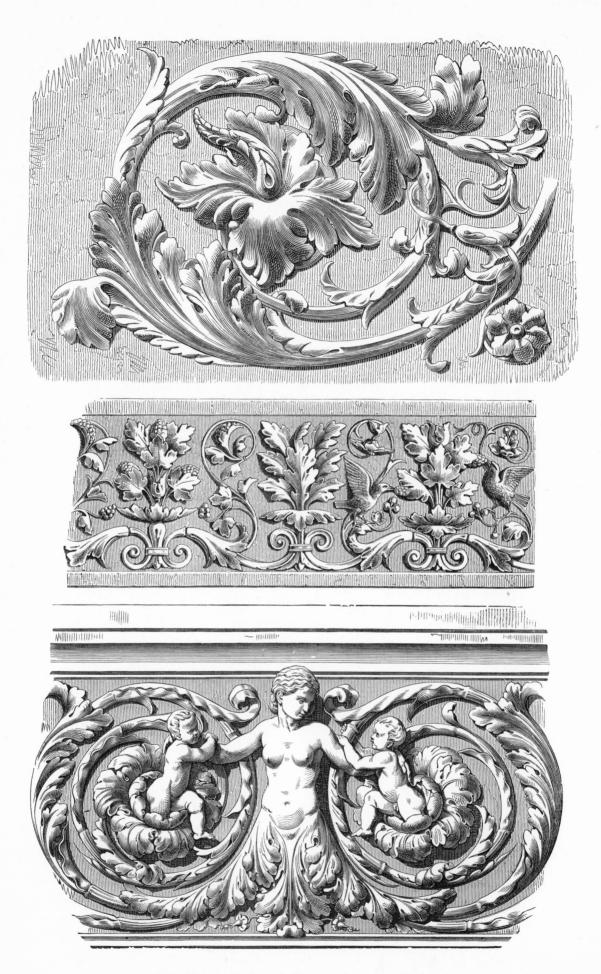

138 Ornaments from Italian Renaissance architecture.

139 Italian Renaissance. ABOVE LEFT: Marble stoup in the Pisa cathedral. ABOVE RIGHT: Fountain in S. Marco, Florence. CENTER: Fountain in S. Croce, Florence.

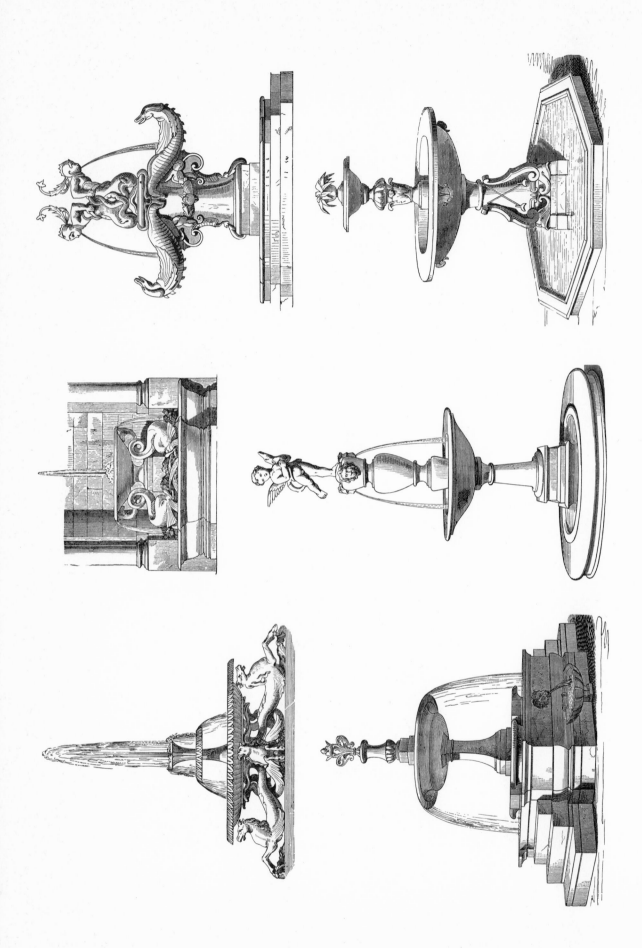

140 Italian Renaissance fountains. ABOVE, LEFT TO RIGHT: Villa Borghese, Rome; Rome; Piazza Annunziata, Florence. BELOW, LEFT TO RIGHT: Piazza S. Croce, Florence; Palazzo Vecchio, Florence; Palazzo Gondi, Florence.

141 Italian Renaissance ship's mast finials of hammered sheet metal, partially in openwork, formerly gilded, from the Morosini palace, Venice.

142 ABOVE, SIDES: Lion's heads from Ghiberti's bronze door of the Baptistery in Florence (15th century). BELOW: Italian Renaissance bronze fireplace fender in the Victoria and Albert Museum, London (16th century).

143 Italian Renaissance. CENTER: Cast-iron fireplace fender in the Museo Nazionale, Florence. SIDES: Knockers from Venice.

144 Bronze grille in the Prato cathedral (15th century).

145 LEFT: Detail of the grille in the Prato cathedral. RIGHT: Wrought-iron grilles from Venice (late 15th century, above; 16th century, below).

146 Wrought-iron and brass entrance grille to the high altar of St. Mary's at Riva (16th century).

147 ABOVE: Fanlight grille in Florence (16th century). BELOW: Grille from S. Anastasia in Verona (16th century).

148   Wrought-iron balcony railings (16th century). ABOVE: From a building on St. Mark's Square, Venice. BELOW: From the palace of Marchese Castiglione in Milan.

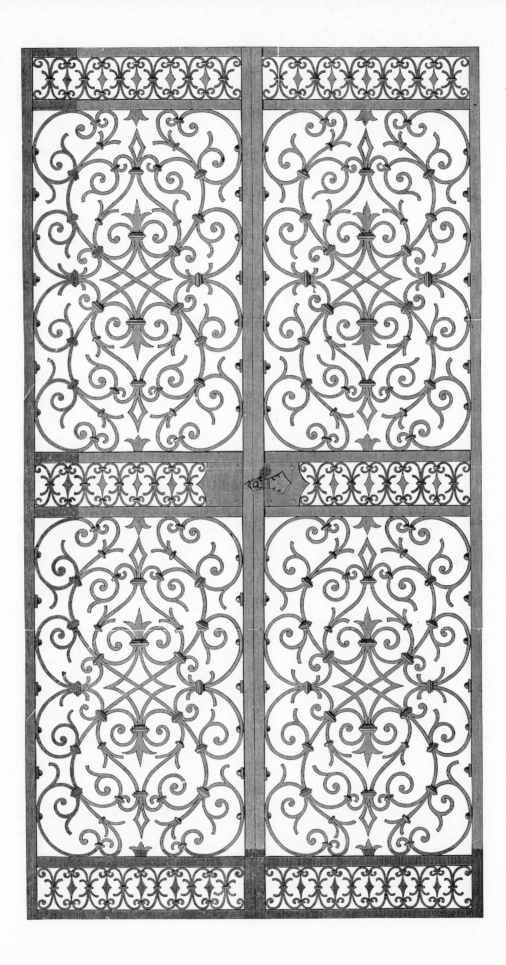

149 Italian Renaissance wrought-iron doorway grille from S. Croce in Florence.

150 Italian Renaissance bronze candelabrum by Maffeo Olivieri in St. Mark's, Venice.

151 Italian Renaissance. LEFT: Candlestick from the collection of drawings in Florence.
RIGHT: Bronze altar candlestick from S. Giorgio in Verona.

152   Italian Renaissance. CENTER: Bronze crucifix from the high altar of the charterhouse near Pavia, 53 inches tall. SIDES: Details of candelabra in Italian museums.

153 LEFT TO RIGHT: Bronze candelabrum of the late 16th century; ciborium, from a
drawing in the Uffizi, Florence; altar candlestick in the charterhouse near Pavia
(17th century).

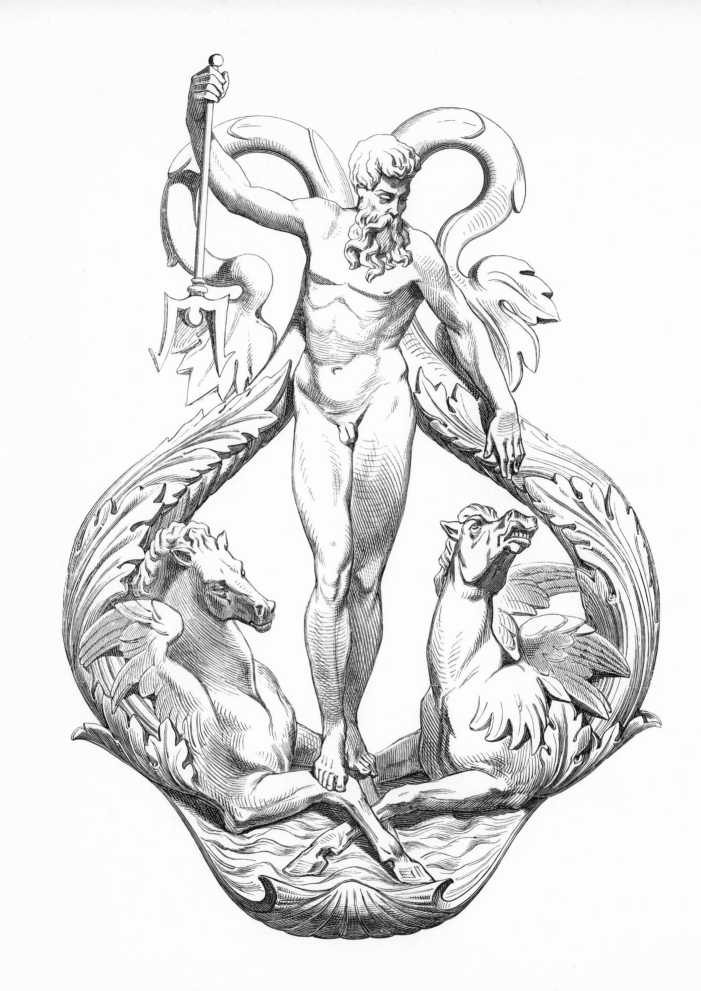

154 Early Italian Renaissance bronze knocker from the Trevisan palace in Venice.

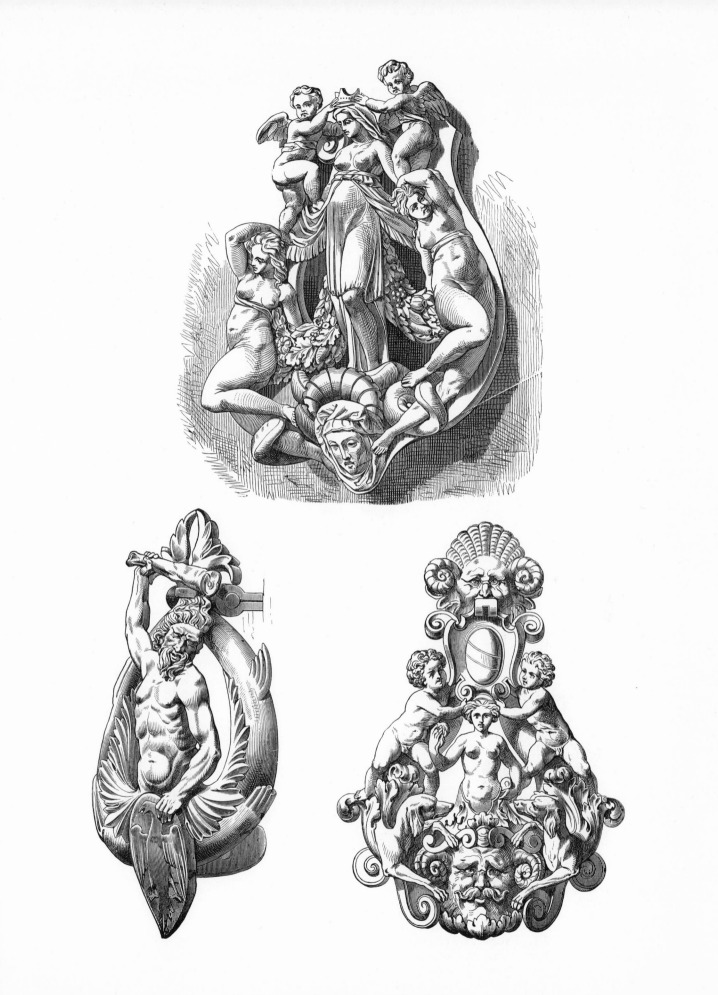

155 Italian Renaissance knockers.

156   Italian Renaissance knockers. TOP, LEFT TO RIGHT: Strada S. Stefano, Bologna;
Palazzo Bevilacqua, Bologna; Strada delle Asse, Bologna. CENTER, LEFT TO RIGHT:
Borgo S. Croce, Florence; Österreichisches Museum; Strada delle Asse, Bologna.
BOTTOM, LEFT TO RIGHT: Strada S. Mamolo, Bologna; door of the pulpit, S. Croce,
Florence.

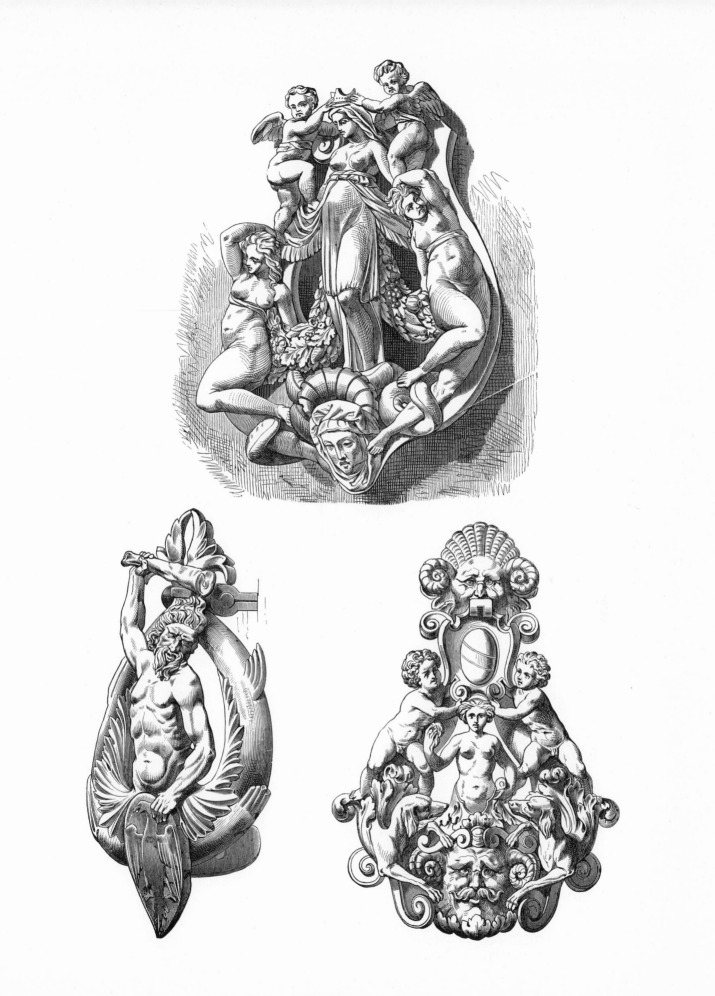

155 Italian Renaissance knockers.

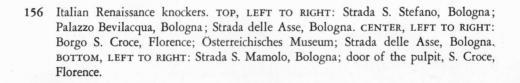

156 Italian Renaissance knockers. TOP, LEFT TO RIGHT: Strada S. Stefano, Bologna; Palazzo Bevilacqua, Bologna; Strada delle Asse, Bologna. CENTER, LEFT TO RIGHT: Borgo S. Croce, Florence; Österreichisches Museum; Strada delle Asse, Bologna. BOTTOM, LEFT TO RIGHT: Strada S. Mamolo, Bologna; door of the pulpit, S. Croce, Florence.

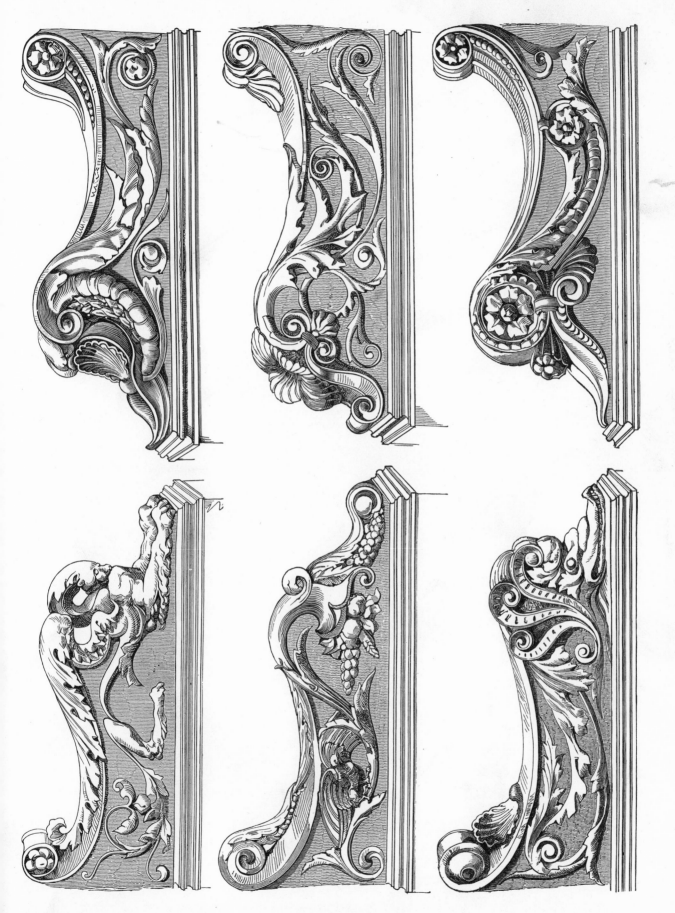

157   Arm rests from the choir stalls of S. Agostino in Perugia (16th century).

158   Wall decoration and desk from the Cambio in Perugia (ca. 1500).

159 CENTER: Panel from the choir stalls of S. Pietro in Perugia (16th century). LEFT
AND RIGHT: Panels from the Cambio in Perugia (ca. 1500).

160   Carved wooden panels from the loggias of the Vatican in Rome (16th century).

161   Carved wooden panel from a door in the loggias of the Vatican.

162 Italian Renaissance. ABOVE: Carved wooden pilaster capitals in the chapel of the
Palazzo Vecchio in Florence. BELOW: Rosettes and frieze from the door of the
church of Madonna di Galliera in Bologna.

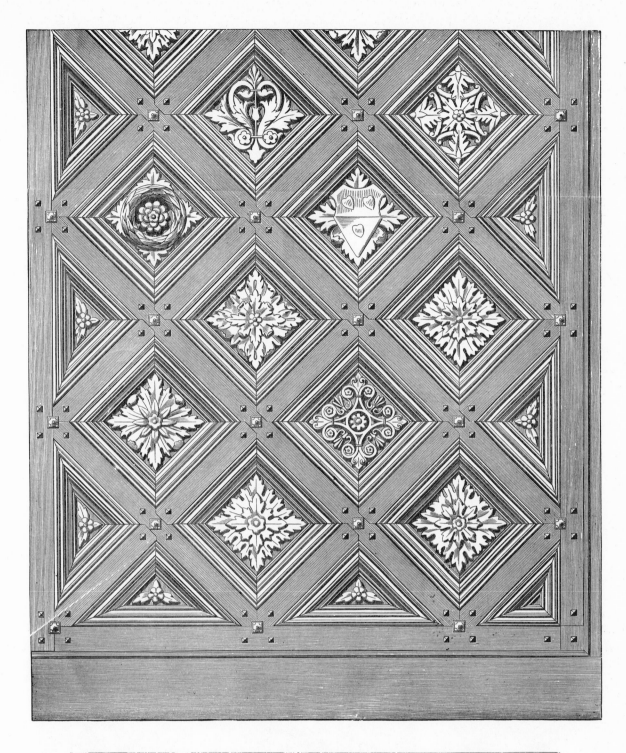

163 ABOVE: Italian Renaissance door of the Cappella Colleoni in Bergamo. BELOW:
Enamel painting on yellow glass in the treasury of St. Mark's in Venice (15th
century).

164 TOP, LEFT AND RIGHT: Rosettes from works of Filippo Brunelleschi. IN BOXES: Rosettes from the door of the Baptistery in Parma.

165   Italian Renaissance. ABOVE: Door of the Baptistery in Parma. BELOW: Ornament
from the church of the Eremitani in Padua.

166   Italian Renaissance. ABOVE: Ceiling element from the Doge's Palace in Venice, carved wood without gilding. BELOW LEFT: Vault painting in a vestibule of the Via Nuova in Genoa. BELOW RIGHT: Vault painting in the Palazzo Spinola in Genoa.

167   ABOVE: Italian Renaissance frame. BELOW: Ceiling of a room in the Doge's Palace
in Venice, gilded carved wood on a blue field (16th century).

168 ABOVE: Ceiling of S. Maria dei Miracoli in Venice (1480). BELOW: Grotesque ornament from Mantua by Giulio Romano (16th century).

169 CENTER: Italian early Renaissance double door, with wood inlays, from the left aisle of S. Lorenzo in Florence, begun by Brunelleschi in 1425. LEFT: Inlay from the double door. RIGHT: Intarsia inlay from the choir stalls of S. Maria in Organo, Verona (1499).

170 BELOW, LEFT AND RIGHT: Details from the door in S. Lorenzo, Florence, shown on the preceding plate. ABOVE: Intarsia inlays from the choir stalls of S. Maria in Organo, Verona.

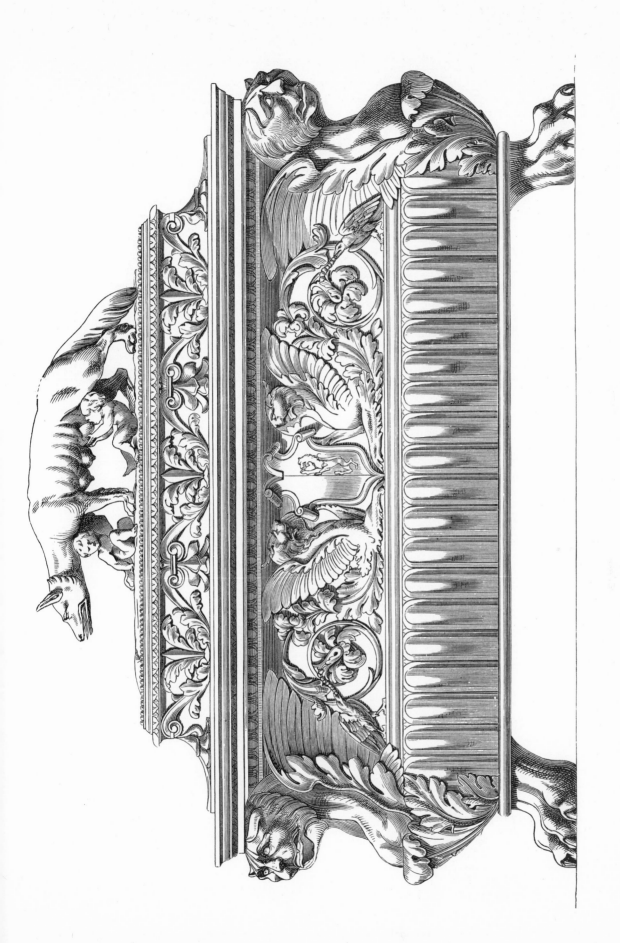

171 Carved walnut box, partially gilded, by Barile in the Palazzo Pubblico, Siena (15th century).

172　Florentine carved walnut box in the Victoria and Albert Museum, London (16th century).

173 TOP: Frieze from a sarcophagus by the Florentine Francesco di Simone in S. Francesco, Bologna. NEXT ROW, LEFT TO RIGHT: Carved panel from the Cambio in Perugia (ca. 1500); carved panel from the Prince's art collection in Sigmaringen. NEXT ROW: Intarsia frieze by Baccio d'Agnolo from the choir stalls of S. Maria Novella in Florence (late 15th century); intarsia panel from the charterhouse near Pavia. BOTTOM: Ornament from the choir stalls of S. Pietro in Perugia (ca. 1535).

174   Low-relief ornaments from Italian Renaissance architecture.

175 Inlaid wood ornaments from the Cambio in Perugia (16th century).

176   Lower half of one wing of the so-called Dante Door, with intarsia ornaments, by
Benedetto da Maiano in the Palazzo Vecchio, Florence (15th century).

177 CENTER: Intarsia ornament from a chapel door in the Palazzo Riccardi, Florence, built in 1440. SIDES: Intarsia ornaments from the sacristy of S. Croce, Florence (late 15th century).

178   Intarsia ornaments from S. Petronio in Bologna (1495).

179   Intarsia ornaments by Antonio Mercatello in the Cambio, Perugia (ca. 1500).

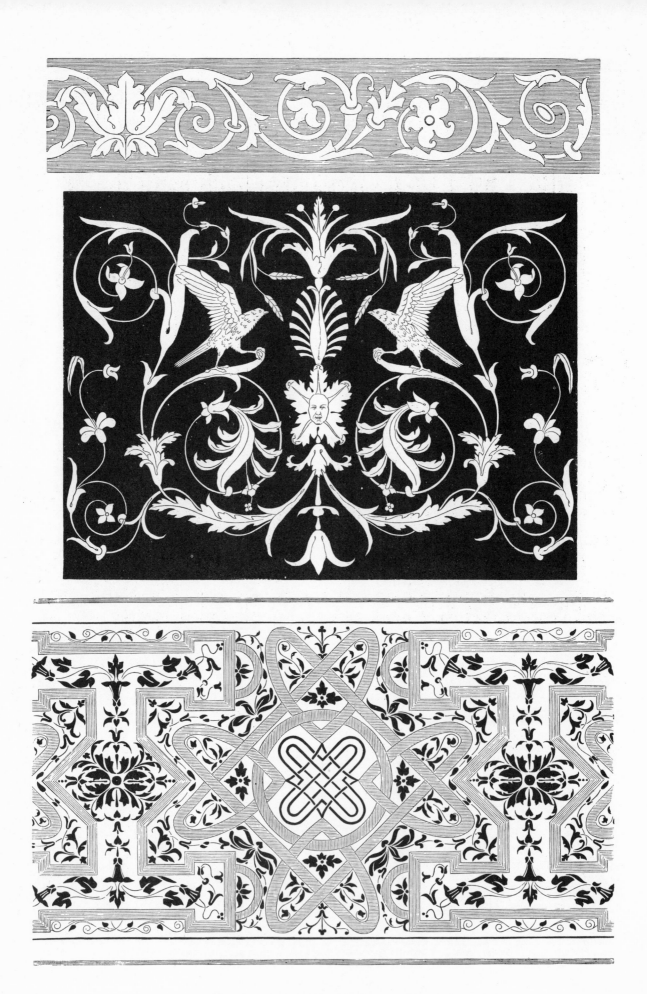

180 Intarsias from S. Maria in Organo, Verona (late 15th century).

181 Inlaid wood from the choir stalls of S. Maria dei Frari, Venice (15th century).

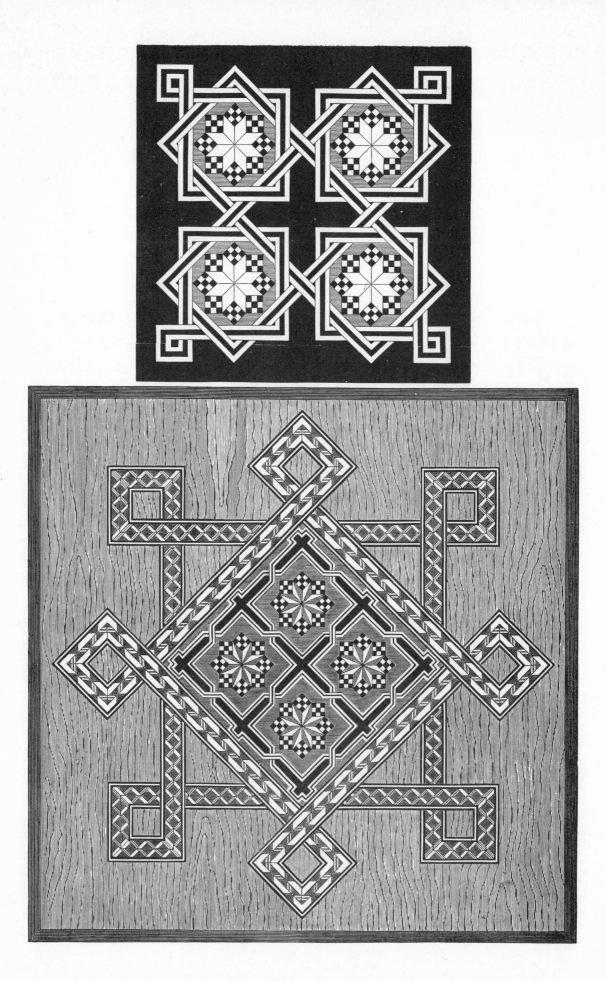

182 Italian Renaissance wood mosaics from S. Anastasia and S. Nazzaro in Verona.

183   Italian late Renaissance panel from a chest in the Museo Correr, Venice.

184　Italian Renaissance borders from marble gravestones in S. Zaccaria and S. Maria dei Frari, Venice.

185 Italian Renaissance mosaic covering of the base of the choir in the charterhouse near Pavia.

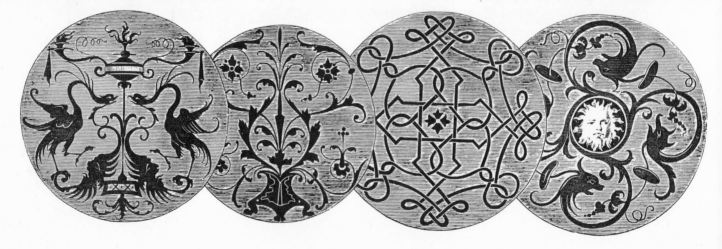

186 Majolica floor from the Oratorio of St. Catherine in Siena (1405–1520).

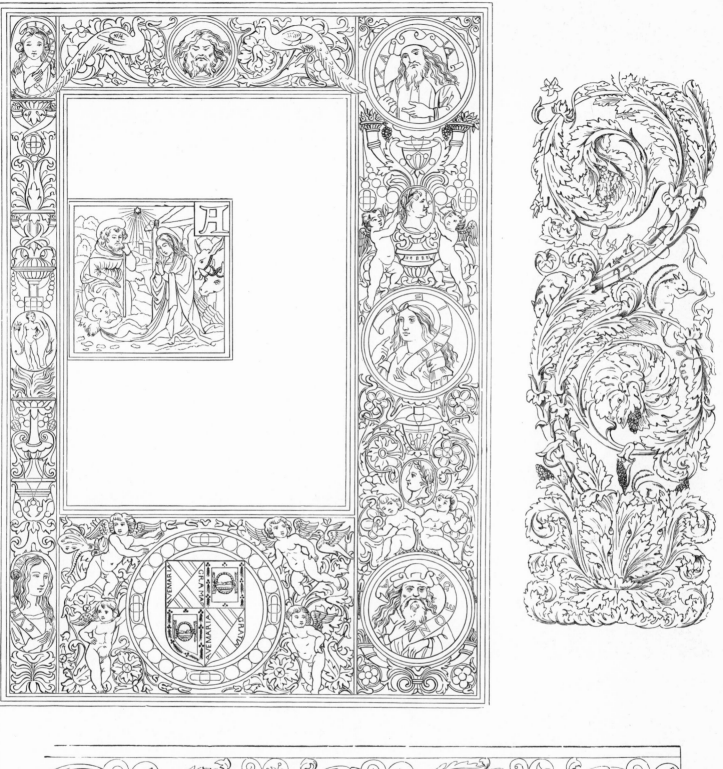

187 ABOVE LEFT: Italian Renaissance book illumination. ABOVE RIGHT AND BOTTOM: Grotesque ornaments from Raphael's Vatican loggias (16th century).

PORTAM·ET·VIAM·PI
AS·PVBLICAE·COMMO
DITATI·APERVIT·ET
MVNIVIT·

188   Ornaments from Raphael's Vatican loggias.

189   Ceiling in the Ducal Palace in Mantua (1527).

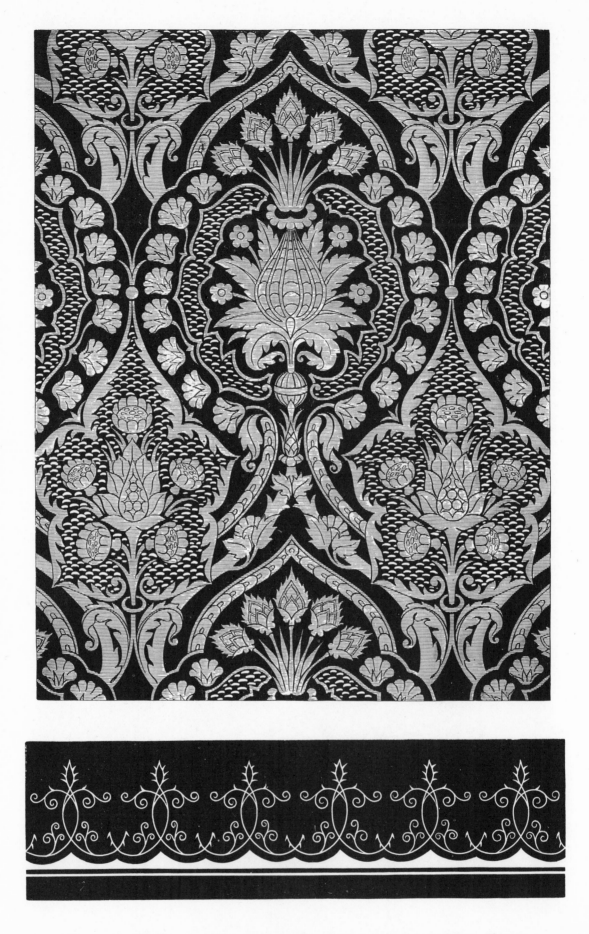

190 ABOVE: **Textile pattern from an antependium (altar hanging) in S. Spirito, Florence.**
BELOW: **Painted edging on a wooden statue in the Ambras collection in Vienna (16th century).**

191 German Renaissance. ABOVE, EXTREME LEFT AND RIGHT: Panels from the Waldemir fountain in Regensburg (16th century). ABOVE, CENTER: Two ornaments of the 16th century. BELOW: Lead relief of the 15th century.

192 Lead reliefs, German Renaissance ornament molds. ABOVE: 16th century. BELOW: 15th century.

193   German Renaissance ornamental panels of the 16th century.

194 TOP: Hem of the tunic on the statue of Count Heinrich of Württemberg in the collegiate church in Stuttgart (1574). NEXT THREE ROWS: Garment hems from funerary monuments in Niederstetten and Lensiedel (16th century). BOTTOM: Renaissance style garment edging, red on a blue field, from the Dutch tapestries in the domed hall of the Dresden gallery.

195   LEFT: Two ornaments from pedestal bases in the former summer house in Stuttgart
(16th century; see Plate 199). RIGHT, ABOVE: Tile in the Germanisches Museum
(16th century). RIGHT, BELOW: Detail of a column of the Nördlingen town hall
(17th century).

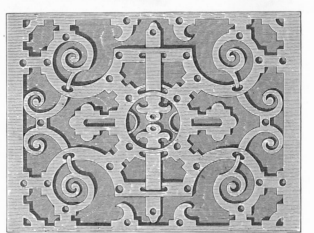

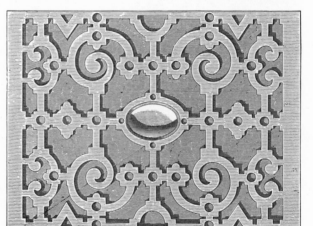

196 German Renaissance. EXTREME LEFT AND RIGHT: Pilaster decorations from the portal of the church at Freinsheim in the Palatinate. CENTER: Three ornaments from Comburg near Schwäbisch Hall.

197   Inner face of an arch at the main entrance of the Otto-Heinrich section of the
       Heidelberg castle (1556–1559).

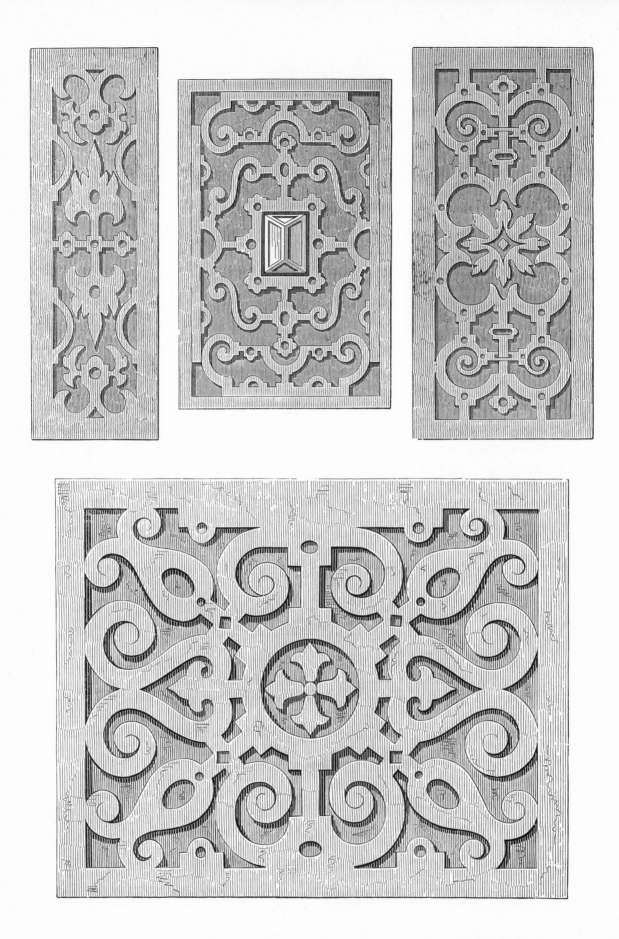

198 ABOVE, LEFT AND RIGHT: Two Renaissance ornaments from St. Michael's in Schwäbisch Hall. ABOVE, CENTER: Renaissance ornament from a funerary monument at Comburg (late 16th century). BELOW: Renaissance panel from the Nördlingen town hall (1621).

199   Renaissance escutcheons from the former summer house in Stuttgart, built by Behr
1580–1593, demolished 1845.

200   ABOVE: Three borders from stamped leather bindings in the Schwäbisch Hall town hall library (16th century). BELOW: Three panels from funerary monuments of the Counts of Württemberg in the collegiate church at Stuttgart (late 16th century).

201 ABOVE: Carpet pattern from a funerary monument in the collegiate church at Comburg (early 17th century). BELOW: Textile pattern from a painting by Albrecht Dürer (16th century).

202   ABOVE: Border from a picture by Domenico Zampieri, called Domenichino (late
16th century). BELOW: Patterned background of stained-glass window from St.
Michael's in Schwäbisch Hall (late 15th century).

203   German Renaissance textile pattern.

204 ABOVE: Pattern of a garment in a picture by Hans Burgkmair (1473–1531).
BELOW: Garment pattern from the monument of Margravine Ursula of Baden in
the castle church at Pforzheim (mid-16th century).

205   Ornament from a stamped parchment book cover of 1554.

206   German Renaissance stamped book-cover ornaments in the Germanisches Museum, Nuremberg.

207　ABOVE: Majolica vase from the Palazzo del Podestà in Florence. BELOW: Stoneware wine cooler in the Nationalmuseum, Munich (late 16th century).

208 ABOVE: German Renaissance stoneware beaker in the Germanisches Museum, Nuremberg (16th century). BELOW LEFT: Crystal goblet in the art collection of Prince Karl Anton of Hohenzollern-Sigmaringen (16th century). BELOW RIGHT: Crystal wine glass in the Nationalmuseum, Munich (17th century).

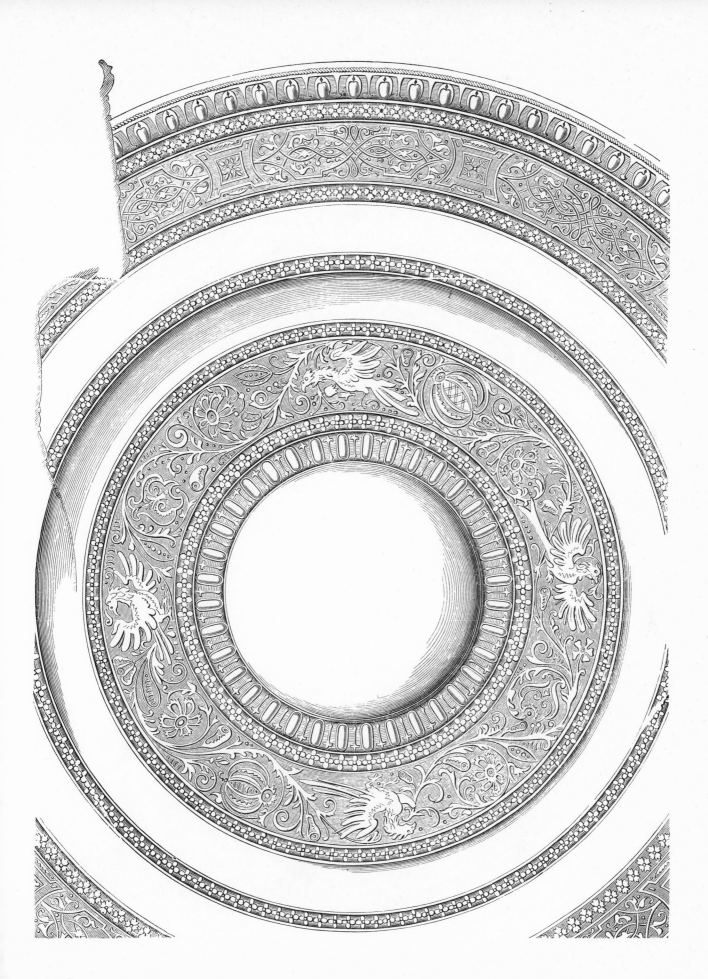

209 Pewter dish made in Nuremberg in the 16th century, in the Nationalmuseum, Munich.

210　Front view and cross section of a gilded salver of the 16th century.

211 Pewter plate in the Nationalmuseum, Munich (17th century).

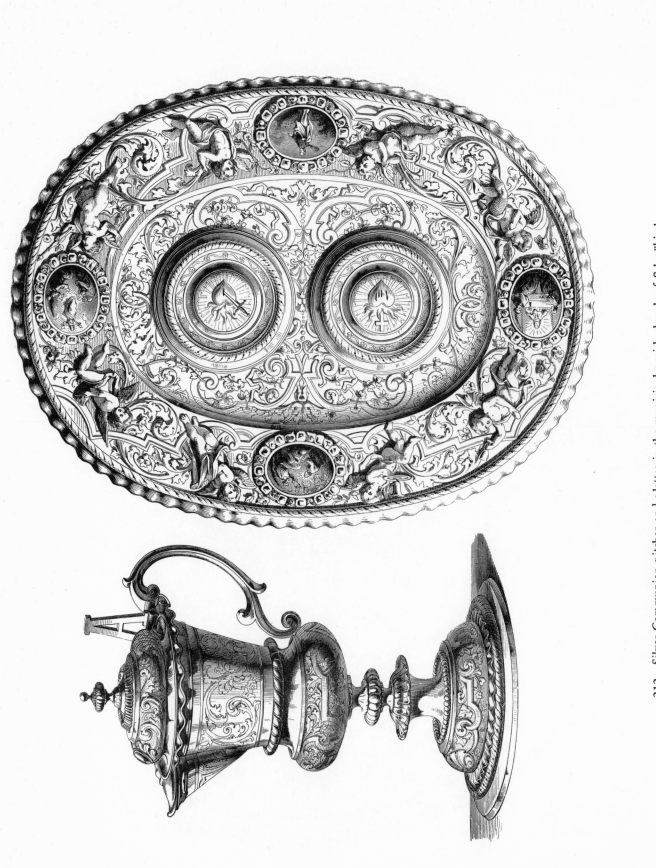

212 Silver Communion pitcher and platter in the municipal parish church of Schwäbisch Gmünd (2nd half of the 16th century).

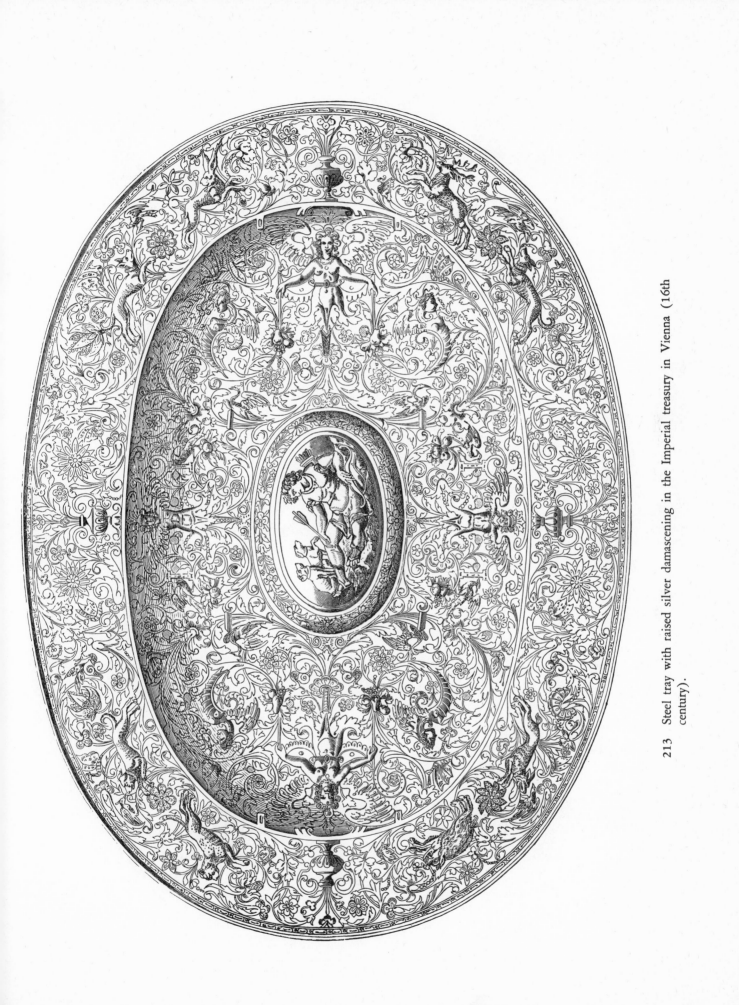

213 Steel tray with raised silver damascening in the Imperial treasury in Vienna (16th century).

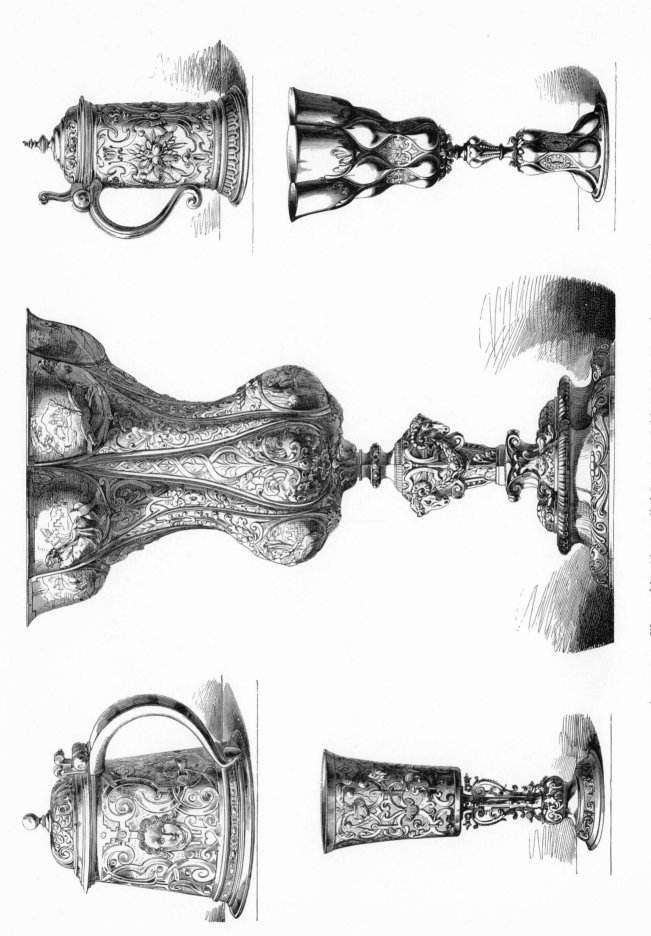

214 CENTER: Silver goblet (the so-called Jamnitzer Goblet) in the Nuremberg municipal collection (16th century). SIDES: Silver drinking vessels from the "Regensburg silver hoard" (16th and early 17th centuries).

215 BELOW, CENTER: Renaissance goblet of the 2nd half of the 16th century, from an old woodcut. ABOVE AND SIDES: Silver drinking vessels from the "Regensburg silver hoard."

216 CENTER: Corner of a book binding in the Royal Library in Munich (1566). SIDES: Coats-of-arms.

217   ABOVE: Raised and damascened helmet in the Austrian Museum of Art and Industry
(17th century). BELOW: Silver gilt vessel in the Ambras collection, Vienna.

218 LEFT: German Renaissance copper tankard in the art collection of Prince Karl Anton of Hohenzollern-Sigmaringen. RIGHT: Raised copper wine pitcher of the Kaschau shoemakers' guild.

219 German Renaissance silver gilt pitcher in the Dresden silver collection.

220 Silver gilt stirrup bottle made in Augsburg in the late 16th century, in the Dresden "Green Vault."

221 Cutlery in the royal and private collections in Dresden (17th century).

222 Tin-plated wrought-iron keyhole plate and hinge from the Augsburg town hall (early 17th century).

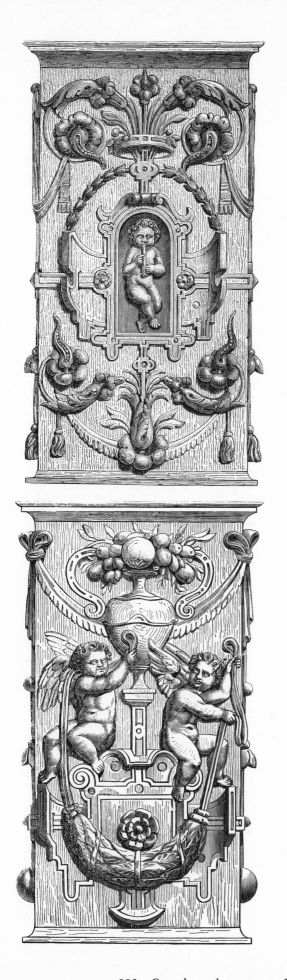

223 Carved wood ornaments from the Mainz cathedral (16th century).

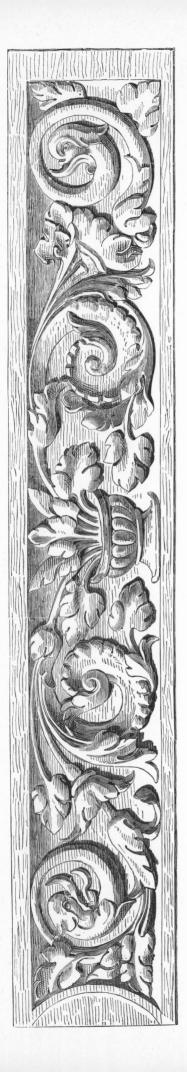

224 Carved wood friezes in the Bavarian National Museum, Munich (early 16th century).

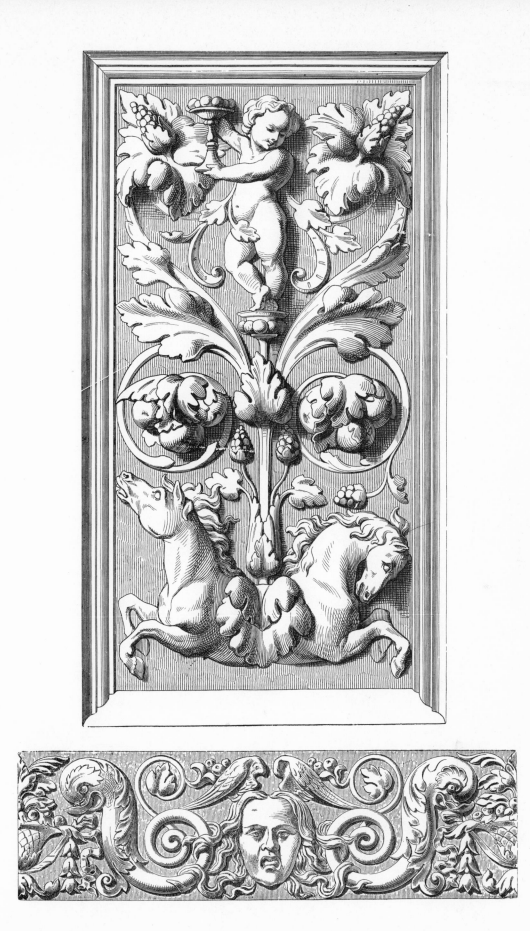

225 ABOVE: Carved wood panel from the porch door of the town hall of Oudenarde, Belgium, made by Paul van der Schelde in 1530. BELOW: German Renaissance ornament of the 16th century.

226   Wooden ceiling from Quedlinburg (1560).

227   Intarsia panels from the choir stalls of St. Mary Magdalene's in Breslau (16th century).

228 ABOVE LEFT: Two Renaissance table legs. ABOVE RIGHT: Table from Husth, Hungary. BELOW LEFT: Two benches from the Bargello museum, Florence. CENTER: Table from St. John's hospital in Bruges (1624). BELOW RIGHT: Table from the cathedral, St. Sauveur, in Bruges.

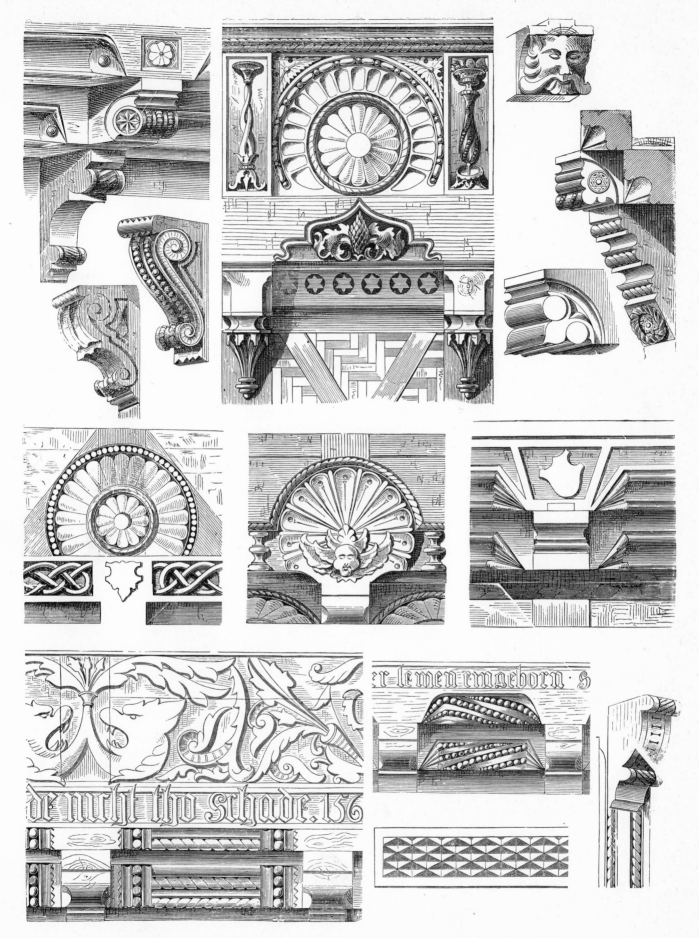

229 Ornaments from wooden buildings in Braunschweig, Halberstadt and Höxter (1530–1575).

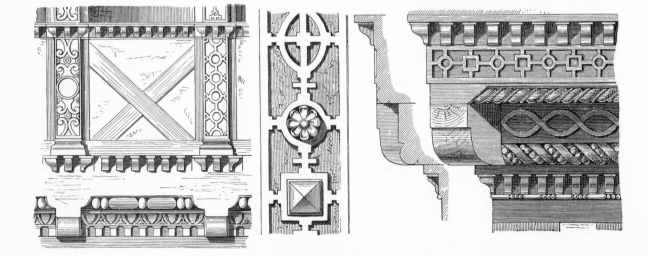

230 Ornaments from wooden houses in Braunschweig, Halberstadt and Höxter (17th century).

231 ABOVE: Door panel from the Brodhaus in Dinkelsbühl. BELOW: German Renaissance console from the Belvedere in Prague.

232   TOP: Two cartouches from a Dutch mirror frame in the Nationalmuseum, Munich.
CENTER: Inlaid work, from a woodcut of 1575. BOTTOM: Panel of a wardrobe in
the Germanisches Museum, Nuremberg (16th century).

233 Table top of jacaranda and ebony with engraved ivory inlays (17th century).

234   Intarsia from the choir stalls of St. Catherine's in Kremnitz, Hungary (1620).

235   LEFT: Wrought-iron grille from a house in Regensburg (early 16th century).
      RIGHT: Wrought-iron window grille from Botzen (16th century).

236 ABOVE: Wrought-iron window grille from a residence in Eperies, Hungary (16th century). BELOW: Wrought-iron grille, after a work by the Salzburg ironsmith M. Georg Klain (1st half of the 17th century).

237 Wrought-iron fanlight grilles. TOP: From Nuremberg (16th century). CENTER AND BOTTOM: From the Nuremberg town hall (17th century).

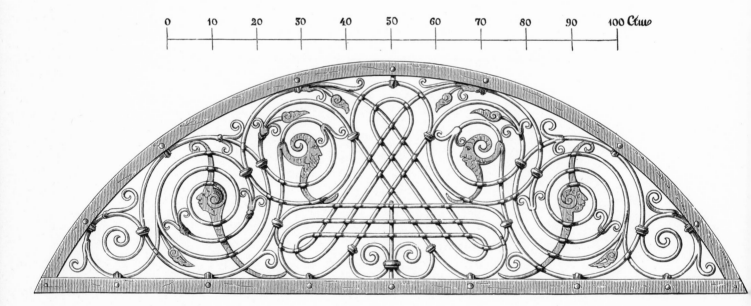

238 Wrought-iron fanlight grilles in the small Bergau palace near Nuremberg (16th century).

239   TOP: Wrought-iron gargoyle bracket from the old palace in Stuttgart (16th century).
CENTER: Bronze knocker from the New Church in Wolfenbüttel (1646). BOTTOM:
Wrought-iron grille panel from the choir of St. Blasius' at Mühlhausen, Thuringia
(1640).

240 TOP: Wrought-iron fanlight grille from the Urban tower in Kaschau, Hungary (1550). CENTER: Wrought-iron grille from the old palace in Stuttgart (16th century). BOTTOM: Wrought-iron door grille, after a work by M. Georg Klain in Salzburg (1st half of the 17th century).

241 ABOVE: Wrought-iron fanlight grille from Frankfurt a. M. (17th century). BELOW: Wrought-iron grille in the Braunschweig cathedral.

242 ABOVE: Two wrought-iron balcony railings from the staircase towers of the royal palace in Dresden (17th century). BELOW: Wrought-iron grille from St. Vitus' in Prague (17th century).

243   Wrought-iron grille from the Strahov seminary in Prague.

244 LEFT: Stairway railing from the house "Zum Alten Limpurg" in Frankfurt a. M.
(16th century). RIGHT, ABOVE: Wrought-iron door vent from St. Salvator's, Prague.
RIGHT, BELOW: Wrought-iron window grille from the parish house of St. Dionysius'
in Esslingen (17th century).

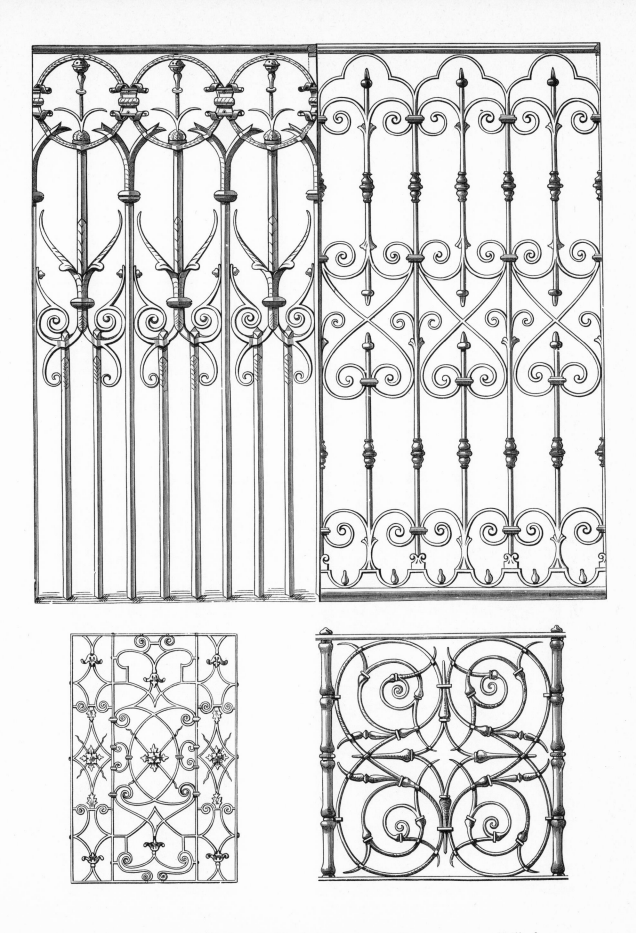

245   ABOVE LEFT: Grille from St. Mary's in Danzig (1620). ABOVE RIGHT: Grille from St. Loretto in Prague (1680). BELOW LEFT: Grille from the town hall in the Old Town, Prague (1680). BELOW RIGHT: Grille from the round tower in Copenhagen (1643).

246   TOP: Wrought-iron grille panel of a fanlight in Prague (17th century). CENTER: Gilded grille of wrought-iron rods in front of a statue of the Madonna near Ponti de' Greci in Venice. BOTTOM: Wrought-iron grille, from a drawing by M. Georg Klain in Salzburg (17th century).

247 ABOVE: Two wrought-iron grilles from a former mortuary chapel in St. Mary's at Lübeck (mid-17th century). BELOW: Two late Renaissance wrought-iron grille panels from the Strahov seminary in Prague.

248 Wrought-iron grilles, from works by M. Georg Klain in Salzburg (1st half of the 17th century).

249   Wrought-iron grilles, from drawings by M. Georg Klain in Salzburg.

250 Grille panels of wrought-iron rods from a courtyard gate in Stuttgart (17th century) . .

251 Wrought-iron grilles, from works by M. Georg Klain in Salzburg.

252　Wrought-iron grilles, from works by M. Georg Klain in Salzburg.

253   German Renaissance wrought-iron sign of the Gray Wolf inn in Regensburg.

254 Fanlight grille from a house in Botzen.

255 Wrought-iron garden gate from the Belvedere palace in Vienna (17th century).

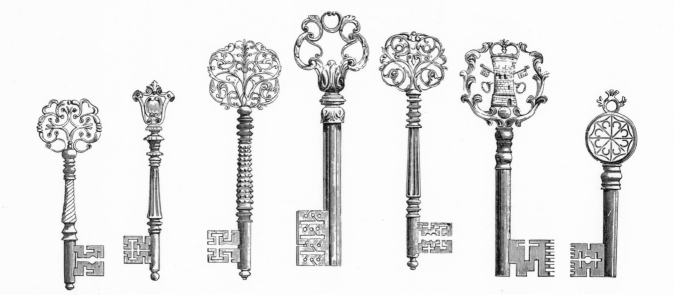

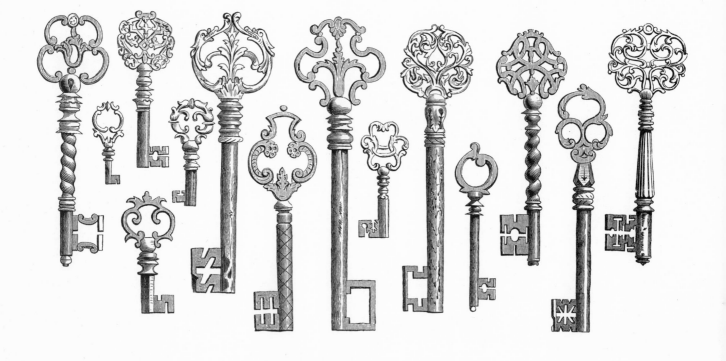

256 German Renaissance latch and keys.

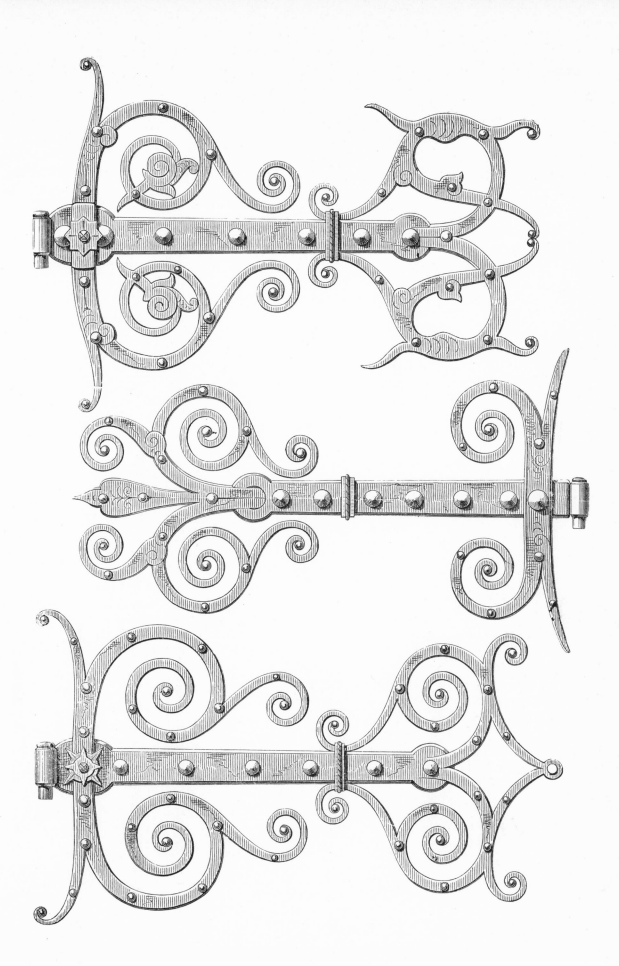

257 Wrought-iron hinges from the old merchants' house on the Limmat in Zurich (1618).

258 Door, wainscoting and wall panel from the Henri II room in the Louvre, Paris
(mid-16th century).

259 Upper part of the white and gold dado from the room in the preceding plate.

260 ABOVE: Panel from the portal of St. Eustache in Paris (16th century). BELOW LEFT:
Two panels in Henri III style (16th century). BELOW RIGHT. Two panels in the
Louvre, Paris (16th century).

261 Window cornice and frieze of the Henri II period, in the Louvre, Paris (mid-16th century).

262 Wood carvings from the choir of the church at Essômes, Aisne (1540).

263 Wood carvings from the choir of the church at Essômes.

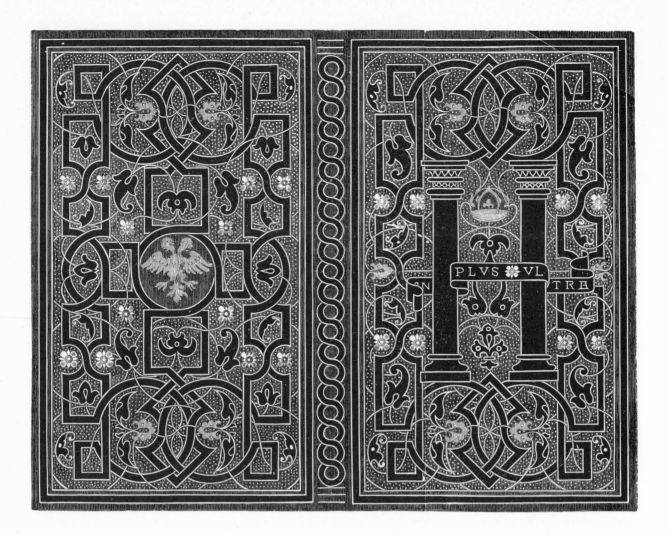

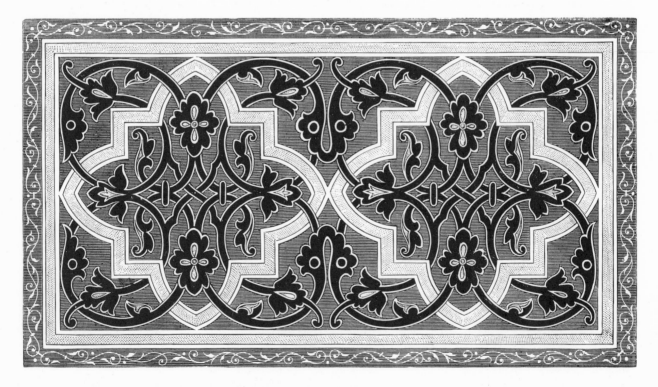

264   ABOVE: Leather binding, stamped in gold, of a parchment manuscript in the
Imperial Library, Vienna (16th century). BELOW: French Renaissance leather book
cover in the Victoria and Albert Museum, London (1551).

265   Patterns of textiles made in Lyons (16th and 17th centuries).

0 5 10   50   100   200 Ctm.

266 ABOVE LEFT: Console from the Heidelberg castle (early 17th century). ABOVE RIGHT AND BELOW: Pilaster console and fireplace from the so-called house of Agnes Sorel in Orléans (mid-16th century).

267 ABOVE: Window cornice from the former Hôtel Sully (17th century). BELOW: Frieze from the portal of St. Etienne-du-Mont in Paris (16th century).

268 ABOVE: Two rosettes of the Louis XIII period (1610–1643). BELOW: Pilaster capital from the tomb of Louis XII in St. Denis (16th century).

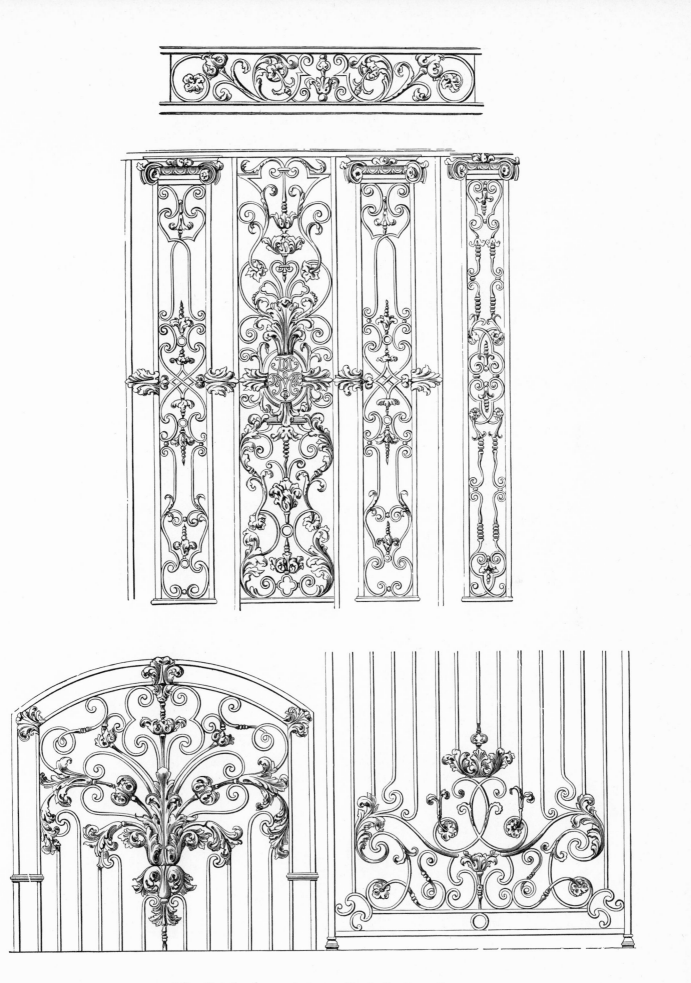

269   Details of wrought-iron grilles in St. Ouen, Rouen.

270 Silk textile from Madrid (17th century).

271 Details of a carved oak door in Paris from the Louis XIV period.

272   Louis XIV table in the old palace at Bercy near Paris.

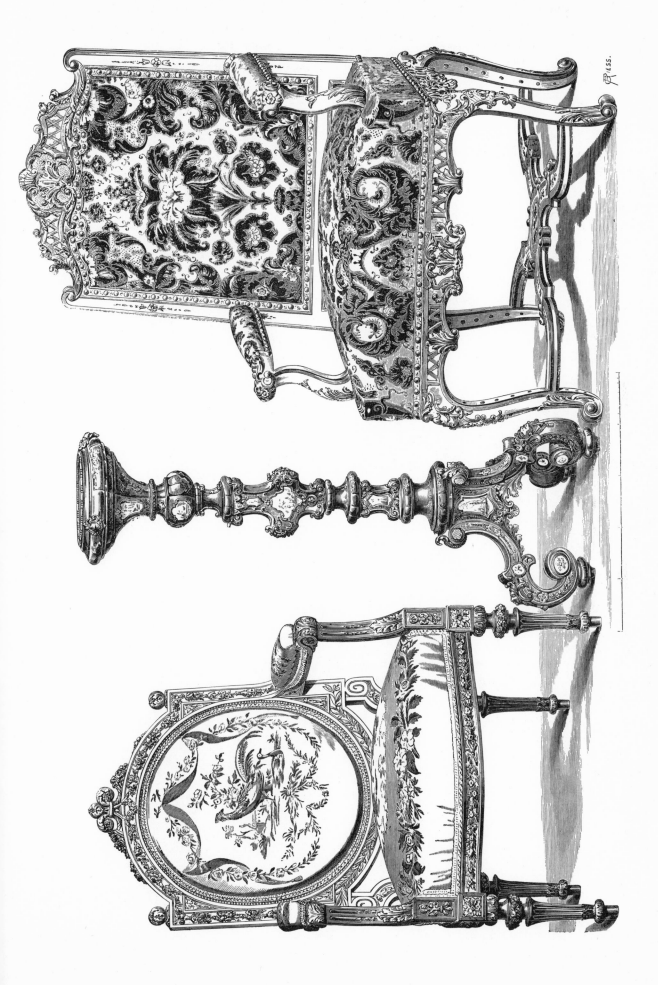

273   Armchairs and pedestal table from the Munich residence (18th century).

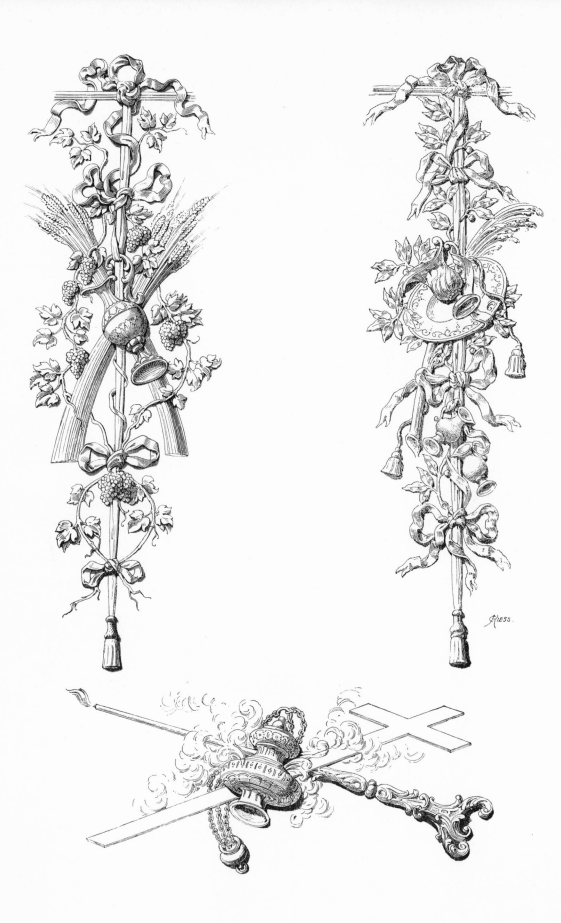

274   Stucco decorations from the palace "Solitude" near Stuttgart (18th century).

275 ABOVE: English fireplace of carved oak and marble (18th century). BELOW: Fireplace of 1710 in the Arts Club, London.

276   Stucco ornaments by Giacomo Albertolli from the ceiling of a room in the palace of the Duke of Milan (18th century).

277　Stucco frieze by Giacomo Albertolli in the Ducal Palace, Milan.

278 Porcelain from the former Imperial factory in Vienna (18th century).

279 Porcelain from the former Imperial factory in Vienna (18th century).

280 Cabinet from the Royal Palace in Madrid, with gilt bronze inlays and painted porcelain tablets (late 18th century).